About th<

Kate Mangold has worked as a corporate event logistics manager for most of her adult life and lives in Surrey.

Her travel stories started as personal memoirs, however, with the twists and turns that her life took, she wanted to share both the good and bad moments that many can relate to so decided to write her first book, *Normal at 40?*

The book is being published around the world.

NORMAL AT 40?

Kate Mangold

Normal at 40?

Vanguard Press

VANGUARD PAPERBACK

© Copyright 2021
Kate Mangold

The right of Kate Mangold to be identified as author of
this work has been asserted by her in accordance with the
Copyright, Designs and Patents Act 1988.

A CIP catalogue record for this title is
available from the British Library.

ISBN 978-1-80016-081-1

*Vanguard Press is an imprint of
Pegasus Elliot MacKenzie Publishers Ltd.*
www.pegasuspublishers.com

First Published in 2021

**Vanguard Press
Sheraton House Castle Park
Cambridge England**

Printed & Bound in Great Britain

Dedication

This book is for my amazing family and friends.
It is a reminder to make the most of what we have,
enjoy every second of life and appreciate the
people that are close to us.
As my auntie says, "Live, Laugh, Love."

The names of everyone in this book have been changed to protect their identity, except that of the author.

Contents

Introduction

Life's too short, as the saying goes, however, when you get to your forties it actually starts to be meaningful and quite scary. In the grand scheme of things, our time here is limited so we should all be making the most of every minute we have — whether we decide to throw our lives into work, travel the world, donate time to helping others or fulfil our own dreams by trying new things and just having fun, we should give everything one hundred per cent as we only get one life so should enjoy it and make the best of it, whatever our circumstances.

Everyone gets on with their own busy lives and our paths are crossed with a huge and diverse amount of people along the way. Inevitably, we all come into contact with people that for some reason make us curious about how we and others live their lives and how our achievements compare with theirs. Suddenly from nowhere, these thoughts may start to arise and a slight panic sets in as we wonder whether we have done enough, pushed ourselves enough and are happy with what we have achieved so far. Maybe we are striving for a perfect life and have it all, or maybe we have let the years pass by just plodding on with our daily routines and then suddenly realising we have nothing to show for our time on this earth — which is so very easily done and it's true what they say about time passing faster when you get older.

For me, curiosity may be misconstrued as sheer nosiness as I like to know in detail about people's lives; what they are doing and how they manage to do it. Whether nosey, curious or both, I use my findings for comparison to my own life's situations and achievements — or under achievements—and to give me ideas on how to manage things better and improve what I do. This is not keeping up with the Jones's or feeling inadequate or wanting likes on social media, but just to spur me on for my own sense of self achievement and nothing to do with anyone else.

Having reached my forties, I suddenly realised that I don't know how my life got to where it is now. Where did the last twenty years go and what have I actually been doing for all those years? There are so many things that I thought I would have done and achieved by now, but somehow time has sped up and here I am, not quite where I had expected to be. I wonder if I should be doing more, or less, to improve the next forty years that I will hopefully be lucky enough to have here and, how will my future achievements match up with others of the same age? Well, it seems there is a great variation in people's lives and achievements and I do believe that a contributing factor of this (but not everything) is where you start from, what you start with and your upbringing, particularly in those crucial teenage years.

People watching, therefore, is obviously a great hobby of mine and I always wonder what people are doing, where they live, where they are going and where they have come from? When I see people of a similar age coming out of beautiful, large, expensive houses I wonder what they do for a living and how they can afford it. Maybe the house was left to them or maybe they own their own successful company? If I see a young person driving an expensive car: is it theirs? Do they have a good job and if so, what is it and how did they get it? Or have they just borrowed the car from their very generous parents? The homeless man that walks past my house every day in all weathers: how did he become homeless? How can he improve his life, and does he want to? Does he like the freedom of no ties and, therefore, chooses to live this way? And then there are the people in the gym during the day when they should surely be at work: how do they manage to have that much free time? Do they work shifts or are they unemployed and, if the latter, then how do they afford the gym membership? I would love to ask everyone questions about how they got to where they are and their day-to-day routines, but obviously that's not the done thing and I think a complete stranger may find me rather intrusive to say the least and also slightly weird.

I sometimes compare my life with what I see around me and wonder if I am doing well or just OK as I have to say that nothing comes easily to me and everything always seems to be a struggle — as I am sure it is for most people even if it doesn't look that way from the outside. Should I have done more with my life and, if so, what, as I am not very creative on the idea front? I have certainly had a full, busy and fun life but maybe not a productive or lucrative one and I will definitely not leave any sort of lasting legacy, but is that a bad thing? I'm sure there must be an element of luck, being in the right place at the right time or even just fate as I do know some people that seem to land on their feet and get great opportunities without putting in much effort at all.

I think I have crammed quite a bit into my life so should I be happy with my lot? For me, these thoughts grow as I get older and close to reaching 'midlife', when you realise that you are running out of what you once thought was never-ending: time.

This book is based on a 'normal' person's life — my life, from teens through to the dreaded forties, or life beginning at forty depending on your point of view. How I got to travel to so many unusual and exciting places and I share some tales of funny experiences along the way. However, I also share some sad moments of the harsh realities of life that many people can relate to including loved ones being hit by severe and very unfair illnesses and how it takes over and completely changes your life and the way you think and prioritise things. Of course, a good story wouldn't be complete without a bit of romance and late-found love — completely real, true life.

I'm sure that it's not just me that wonders about all of these things and how our lives compare to others of a similar age. There is always someone else out there who has a similar challenge, who has been in a similar situation to you even if you think you must be the only person in the world with a particular problem.

Life really is too short and that's not just a phrase but now a way of life to make the most of every minute, so most of all, I want to encourage everyone to 'seize the day' and 'live for now' as none of us know what is around the corner. If you have been thinking about a new venture but not got around to it — do it now if you possibly can. If you have been wanting to try a new activity, sport or hobby but keep putting it off as you think you are too old or you are nervous about failing — just do it now. Want to travel but worried what is out there? Just get out there and find out (with safety in mind of course) — broaden your horizons and get right outside of your comfort zone as it may change the whole way you live and are able to deal with other things in your life and it probably won't be as scary as you thought.

Even if you just make the effort to plan a day trip out with the family for a walk to enjoy a view together, climb a big hill together, helping each other along the way, there really is no better feeling of achievement and success in something big or small that will create great memories. But nothing is worse than the feeling of regret — I wish I had tried it, I wonder what would have happened and where I would be now if I had given it a go?

Even if you try it and don't like it or it doesn't work for you, at least you know you have given it your all.

So finally, I hope the tales of my life so far will give you at least a few laughs, introduce you to some new places to travel to that you may not have thought about and possibly spur you on to get out there and try something new and exciting that you never would have tried without a little push, or even just to make you more content and realise how lucky you are with what you have.

And it may just help me answer my own question:

Am I *Normal at 40*?

Chapter One
A bit about me

Growing up was pretty 'normal', I guess, which isn't the best of descriptive words but my definition of normal is good in my book which is having a stable home with the right amount of discipline, healthy food and love, plus some good friends and a carefree childhood which I know I was very lucky to have.

My family are great, and I think families are very important. I like living close to them all and we speak every week and see each other every few weeks.

My upbringing was with the most fantastic parents who were very loving but also implemented discipline when necessary which I think played a large part in how I turned out and has made me a better person. We didn't have loads of money so there were no luxuries but just the necessities which has given me my respect for earning and especially spending money and, in particular, the value of the possessions I now have.

I was adopted at birth so was lucky to end up with my parents as it could have been a completely different story—again, maybe fate was on my side or maybe I was just lucky.

I have an adopted sister, Jane, who I always got on with tremendously. We had the usual arguments and sisterly fights—some quite rough as I remember shutting Jane's head in a door one time and then I moaned when she pushed me down the stairs in retaliation. No harm done and all part of growing up. All in all, I think I fought my corner quite well as she is older and bigger than me!

Jane is a funny (but lovely) old bean. We are like chalk and cheese. She is an old hippy at heart and at nearly six feet tall; I think she stole my share of height as I am only five feet two (and a half) and her dead straight hair is the complete opposite of my mass of curls. She is married now, to a really nice guy, and they live about half an hour away from me so I see her quite a lot and we always have a Friday night phonecall to catch up on all the week's gossip and exciting things that have happened which, in actual fact, is normally nothing apart from going to work, finding a bargain in the supermarket or seeing a rare bird in the garden. Oh, how things change when you get older. She has had her fair share of challenges along the way but has come out the other side and is very settled and doing well. Her 'alternative' personality has led her from a career in marketing to being a plumber and a fully trained and certified gas engineer, and getting a job as a foreman on a very large building site managing a team of blokes. Well, she is kind of one of the lads. I'm very proud of her as it takes a lot of work and determination, let alone guts, to make a change like that—how fantastic and inspiring.

She has never been one for holding back and says what she thinks. She drinks way too much wine (as do I) and plays her music so loud that I feel sorry for her neighbours and even the people at the other end of the street. Although she is three years older than me, I sometimes wonder if the date on her birth certificate was written down incorrectly as she really doesn't act it. We call each other 'The Gibbons' for some reason—I can't even remember how it started but it has stuck, and everyone that joins our household, whether it be by marriage or close friends, have to become honorary Gibbons, which they all seem to like as it is a term of endearment!

The Gibbon and her husband, Arnold, have a lovely house that Jane bought when it was in not such a good state and being used as a squat that was covered in graffiti, and with a smell too nasty to describe, so she managed to buy it for a very good price. They have both spent years improving it and it is now a cosy home with a lovely garden. She has caught the 'grow your own' bug from our dad and has some splendid plants in a greenhouse that was given to them as a gift and transported to their house on the roof of my dad's very small car—Mr Bean springs to mind—and I'm glad they didn't have to go under any low bridges en route!

Growing up, we all lived at the top of a big hill in a house that had a great garden for running in as it was a corner plot so it wrapped all the way around.

As a family we used to go on really fun holidays to holiday camps, which were all the rage back then, and took part in all the dressing up competitions and all the games that were going on. I was very proud to win a dressing up competition when I dressed up as a Hawaiian hula dancer in a grass skirt made from raffia paper, a flower garland around my neck made of red and yellow crêpe paper and string, and my mum covered me in cocoa powder to make me look suntanned which smelt delicious! Ahh those were the days as I don't think you would get away with entertainment like that now without a Wii or Playstation on hand as back up.

Our mum was a stereotypical housewife (back in the day). She loved being at home and used to always be in the kitchen cooking us up hearty dinners every night with home-grown vegetables straight from the garden, sometimes still left with a bit of dirt on that made that awful crunching sound that left you wondering if a bit of your tooth had fallen out. Amazing tasting runner beans were served up with every meal while in season until they were coming out of our ears and then they were also frozen so they would last the whole year, and the oddest shaped carrots were paraded around the house to make us laugh. We were made to recite our times table before dinner every evening which were written on big sheets of paper and stuck on the dining room walls which I am thankful for now, but not so much at the time.

Mum was lovely—of course. She was so happy with everything she had: a house, a husband and two children. She often used to wear clothes made by my grandma that weren't the most fashionable, however, she was very money conscious so hardly ever bought anything new but didn't mind in the slightest. She used to do the ironing while watching Wimbledon as she loved it but wouldn't sit down to watch it as she always had to be doing jobs.

She was more than happy driving around in our bright yellow 2CV car with its ridiculously thin wheels that made it feel as though it would topple over on every bend. It was a great little car until it was squashed by a very large lorry with our mum in it and it folded in like a tin can. At this point my dad decided to buy something a bit sturdier which I was very relieved about.

Sundays in our house were treat days when we were allowed a small bag of sweets. Oddly enough for a small child, my favourite sweets were aniseed balls and also black jacks as they used to make my tongue go a funny colour which I thought highly amusing and actually still do, although now I have to watch they don't pull my fillings out—oh, how sad! I used to sit on the sofa with my sweets watching the original *Planet of the Apes* series, half hiding my face behind a cushion as it was very scary, but I loved it.

Like many children, I used to sleepwalk. Quite a lot, in fact, and I once freaked my sister out as I had walked downstairs, put the TV on and sat there watching it with my eyes wide open but still asleep—how very creepy is that? I could actually have a conversation with anyone that spoke to me so it was often difficult to tell if I was asleep or not and, once coaxed back to bed by Mum and Dad, I only had a vague recollection of it in the morning. I'm pleased to say I've grown out of it and hope it isn't one of those things that ever comes back as you do hear of adults doing very strange things while sleepwalking...

Our dad is lovely—like a big teddy bear. He doesn't say too much but he is always there if we need him. He is a real home body and doesn't like to go out too often, but instead spends most of his time in the garden tending to his vegetables and flowers, or in the greenhouse potting up seeds, or in the garage making things. He enters the local shows with his flowers and vegetables and has even been in the local newspaper with a picture showing off 'his huge parsnips', much to everyone's amusement. You can see his air force background as everything is so neat, both inside and outside the house. All the seed and flowerpots are lined up with labels facing outward, the garden hose stored neatly with each loop the same size and each type of nut and bolt has its own home-made drawer in the garage. Inside the house is the same with the tea towels lined up to the same length hanging over the towel rail and the food tins in the cupboard all facing labels out—I'm sure there is a horror film like that...

He doesn't buy many clothes and still wears his really old seventies shirts for gardening that he has ripped the sleeves off; my favourite being the one with different shades of brown stripes, very Huggy Bear! Until they actually fall apart then they are still good for wearing, apparently. I have obviously inherited some of this weirdness, or should I really say thriftiness, and still have clothes from twenty years ago that I don't want to throw away. Not that I can't fit in to them any more but you never know, and old jeans with holes in them do make great decorating trousers even if I can't do the button up!

We used to have a little sailing boat that we kept in the back garden with its light blue paint and red sail, named *Kinnel*. A bit rude (you may need to say it slowly and there are a few letters missing from the beginning...). However, as I was young, I hadn't worked this out and actually now wish that I had never been told. It was a mirror dinghy and we used to race it each weekend, which I loved, even after the mast once broke and clonked me on the head which did hurt quite a lot as it was a thick wooden mast. I would always have a fizzy drink and a wagon wheel as a treat after the race and sat at the small bar in the clubhouse afterwards, which was freezing and had loads of massive cobwebs and spiders but also that strangely nice smell of damp that I now find familiar and comforting. Unfortunately, when I got to those teenage years, I would prefer to stay in bed on a Sunday morning rather than lug heavy ropes and a boat around getting cold and wet, which of course I now regret and wished I had carried on. My dad sold the boat which I was very upset about and my dream is to find it and buy it back for him so we could take it out for a few more sails. So if anyone knows of its whereabouts (even though this was over thirty years ago) please let me know!

My sister and I were taught good manners, had fun, and generally had the best upbringing that anyone could wish for thanks to my mum and dad. Everything in our life was very stable which is more than can be said for a lot of children nowadays, which definitely has an effect on their outcome.

My school days were OK—I didn't 'shine' or show any amazing potential but just did what I needed to do to get by. I probably could have done much better if I had applied myself more, however, at that age, I was not aware of the future implications of minimal qualifications, how much harder it would be for me in later life and how many less options and choices I would have available. But that's all so boring at that age and I now sound like a really old person! Hindsight is a wonderful thing.

At secondary school there were four of us that used to hang out together and we were virtually inseparable for years so grew up together, spending all day at school and also all of our spare time together at each other's houses but mostly at the girl's house who looked after horses so we could have a ride from time to time. I remember she once rode up to my dad's house and parked her horse on the drive next to the front door where it instantly had a big poop which my dad loved as he shovelled it onto the garden to feed the plants! As we got a bit older, the other three all started smoking which, luckily, I chose not to do, partly due to laziness as I couldn't be bothered to keep moving my hand up to my mouth, and partly because I didn't really know how to inhale the smoke and even just breathing in the fumes from other people's cigarettes made me cough, plus the smell was horrid. Especially when you had been out for a night with freshly washed hair which then reeked the next day of stale smoke, as in those days you could smoke in pubs and clubs—thank goodness the law changed. However, the worst thing for me was the fact that smoking gave you yellow fingers which I have found can also be an effect from eating too many Twiglets (which I love)—hopefully though they are not quite as bad for you as smoking, but this did put me off eating them without wearing latex gloves as it took days to wash off!

I had a summer job working in a factory packing dolls which was boring but you just got on with it at that age and thought of the money at the end of the week and the other people who worked there were really fun so I made some new friends.

My school friends and I started the whole nightclubbing and drinking thing (normally brandy and Babycham or a Long Island iced tea!) at quite an early age—about fifteen in fact which I know is not considered young these days, but of course, as every teenager does, we used to think we were so grown up by getting into the local nightclub and really believed we looked and acted older than we were and had no trouble being served alcohol. Looking back, it was so obvious we were underage but, in those days, it was different and as long as we were sensible (which we were) then no one seemed to mind. Overall, I think I was lucky to have the friends I did, as we were all pretty good and would never do anything bad, just messed around a bit and had a laugh. We weren't at all grown up for our age and lucky we didn't have to grow up faster due to circumstances so, at fifteen, we were still children. I'm sure it would have been a completely different story if I had fallen in with the 'wrong' crowd, so maybe fate did play a part in shaping my future at a young age.

So, all in all, life was good and we were all very happy and chugging along as a normal family until, one day, we got some life changing and earth-shattering news.

I'm not sure exactly how it happened, and the details are all a bit of a blur, however, one day I just remember my mum sitting Jane and I down on her bed and looking very serious. She started to tell us that she had been diagnosed with leukaemia. Even though we were young teenagers, we knew how serious this was although it didn't seem to sink in that anything bad might actually happen.

Over the next few years, I think we were oblivious to the full extent of the trauma and pain going on in the house and the constant trips to the hospital with awful treatments that our poor mum had to endure, making her sick and losing her hair and generally feeling really ill, mixed in with emotions of sadness and being terrified. It was a roller coaster of all sorts of emotions and feelings and my poor dad started to go a bit greyer, both in hair and complexion, due to the stress which was awful to see; but there was nothing we could do except try to be as good and helpful as possible.

It was when I was seventeen and, following my mum's numerous visits to the hospital, that the leukaemia really took its hold and sadly our mum died; it was the most awful time for all of us, but especially my dad. I have never seen him go such a horrid shade of white, which I never wish to see again.

My sister and I were taken along to the hospital—I don't think you ever forget the sights, sounds and smells of a moment like that, which is not one I care to repeat. We were told that our mum had passed away and asked if we wanted to see her, which my sister did, but I didn't.

I remember that day too clearly; the worst day of my life, and I am sure it will be stuck in my head forever. They say it gets easier with time, but I beg to differ on that one and still get upset when I think or talk about my mum. The following days, weeks and months are all a bit of a blur. I think you go on to autopilot just to get through each day while still in a state of numbness.

Unfortunately, on the following Monday, just a few days after that awful day, I had my driving test booked. Obviously, I wanted to cancel this, however, was encouraged to continue and told that, "Mum would have wanted you to", which you don't argue with. The driving instructor wasn't quite sure what to say when I responded to his question, "Did you have a nice weekend?" Unfortunately, but understandably, I failed my first test.

Our poor dad did an amazing job thereafter. He cooked, cleaned and even ironed for us which seems terrible when you think I was seventeen and my sister twenty, so should have been doing all of this for him, however, in those days, kids didn't grow up so fast and we were both fairly young and immature for our age.

Funny things stick in your head from tough times as I remember, one day, that Dad looked really concerned as he had ironed something for me that shouldn't have been ironed and it had stuck to the iron resulting in a big hole. He looked so worried and said he would buy me a new one. I felt so guilty that he was worried about something like that. I told him not to be silly as it was old and I was going to throw it away anyway.

A few years passed and, as my sister and I were getting older, we were getting more independent and not being at home as much. Dad decided it was time to 'get back out there' for which my sister and I were really proud of him. It's really difficult for anyone to do when you have been happily married for such a long time and thought you were going to spend the rest of your life with one person, let alone our dad who didn't really enjoy going out and socialising.

Our dad has two brothers who have both done very well for themselves, however, our dad is the most grounded one of the three; sensible and reliable which was a great influence on my sister and me. In his day he was an amazing swimmer and cyclist, cycling for miles for a fun day out with his friends and, on one outing, spending the night in a farmer's barn in amongst the haystacks—those were definitely the good old days. He would be a great advert now for healthy living but not so much his fashion sense as I do have a fabulous photo of him sporting an impressive pair of sideburns!

So, finally, our dad did actually meet someone new who is now our stepmother, Ellen. They met through one of his singles groups that he had joined. I have to admit that when we first met Ellen, my sister and I were not the nicest of people and gave poor Ellen a bit of a hard time, because we had lost our mum I guess and didn't want anyone trying to replace her, but we are really glad she stuck around as she is fantastic and certainly keeps my dad on his toes! Ellen has the most incredible memory and always remembers dates of, not just birthdays, but impotant events and also buys great birthday presents as she has really good taste—how shallow we are! Ellen has five children and I have to say it was a bit daunting meeting them all, but they are all lovely too and now all married with children of their own. Christmas time around my dad's house is always a very cosy affair as there are so many people and presents all trying to squash in to not the biggest of spaces but there is always a great atmosphere.

So, my background and upbringing have obviously shaped how I've got to be who I am now, but, even at forty-ish, I still think that I should be learning more, seeing more, doing more and really enjoying life to the full. Most of all I want people to remember me when I'm gone. I don't crave fame like a pop star but would like to leave something behind that I'm known for, although I'm not sure what that is yet and certainly don't want it to be anything bad!

Now in my forties I, am starting to see the usual signs of age, my eyes are already giving up on me, I'm guessing from years of looking at computer screens. I gave in and got a pair of reading glasses when my arms wouldn't extend any further when trying to read menus and magazines and I couldn't see the date on my watch without squinting. My hair is slowly losing its moisture and turning into wire wool and has been going grey since my mid-twenties so I am constantly using home colour kits that, apart from unavoidably spraying most of the bathroom, if you use too many times your hair goes jet black which is not a good look, especially when the grey roots start to creep through so I often look like Morticia Adams. Everything else seems to be intact and in good working order and, so far, defying the laws of gravity but I know it's only a matter of time… Ahhh, what else do I have to look forward to? Failing hearing, which is possibly starting to occur already as I find myself turning my head to use my good ear, but I still tell myself that everyone else is mumbling and try to convince them of it. Varicose veins, teeth falling out— yes, actually on that road already and have spent a small fortune on my teeth (not the veins). And, of course, the menopause is still to come—oh, deep joy, I can't wait! I know that the sayings 'Life begins at forty and 'Life is too short' are definitely applicable to me now and, as none of us know what is around the corner, I think we should all make the most of *now*.

In an effort to keep as healthy as possible, I try to eat good food that some people may see as boring, but I absolutely love. Fresh fish, tasty garden vegetables bursting with flavour and loads of water—yummy—all of which you can feel doing some good as it goes down. Unfortunately, I'm not the greatest of cooks which is a bit limiting and, although I watch a whole host of cooking programmes, I seem to lack the creativity and ability to mix things up, throwing a herb or spice in here and there to produce something amazing as many people can do, but I can follow a recipe and turn out something quite nice if I put my mind to it and have the time. My memory is bad so I can't remember how to cook things, so often end up with quite bland dinners having missed out a vital ingredient unless I follow a recipe word for word, which often takes me hours instead of minutes, although I do have to say I can make a mean cottage pie and bean and vegetable stew! However, my effort at making a chocolate sponge cake (not healthy I know) was interesting as I wasn't sure what the bicarbonate of soda was for and, as I didn't have any, I just left it out. Also having used normal flour and not self-raising flour, my frisby looking sponge cake was greeted with the comment, "Where is the other half?" Lesson learnt.

I'm not a great lover of anything spicy—even salt and vinegar crisps are too hot for me as they strip a layer off my tongue, and I only eat a handful of takeaways per year which are always the same—crispy duck pancakes. Wow, I sound good! However, I'm not as I have the most dreadful chocolate addiction and sometimes—quite often, scoffing a family bar of chocolate to myself within minutes and then still having room for a few malteesers... I love a glass of wine or four, and am always surprised when there is nothing left in the bottle—where does it go? Have they made the bottles smaller or are my wine glasses excessively large? (I think I may have just answered my own question there...) I drink way too much coffee that I justify to myself by offsetting with the occasional decaf, but my favourite drink of all is water! I love plain water which, yes, I know is a bit weird, so feel very righteous when I have drunk my two and a half litre RDA by lunchtime and feel that somehow it offsets all my other bad habits… female logic I like to call it and, of course, you all know that we are always right…!

As for exercise, I do actually do a fair amount when work permits, which means it's a bit sporadic. I love the great outdoors, fresh air and running outside, I go to the gym and like the occasional swim and waterski whenever I can and if it is warm enough. I've tried yoga, Pilates, aerobics body pump and most other classes going. My weight goes up and down, however, now mainly up, but I blame it on sitting down for nine hours a day in the office and then another three in the car which is really not good for you—sounding familiar to anyone?

So, should I be bothered if I put on a few pounds? Surely, it's kind of expected as we grow older isn't it? Well actually no, why should it be the case? I still want to be looking fabulous and be leaping around when I reach one hundred which, by the way, is my goal. I need to try harder to cut down or cut out the choccie as it is way more difficult to shed the pounds as you get older as everything seems to stick to your middle.

I think I need a complete lifestyle change; a new job that doesn't entail sitting down all day with lots of stress that just makes me eat comfort food, and a long journey so I can't make it to the gym after work as I definitely couldn't go before.

Or what about having plastic surgery? Well, that is not for me as I think I would be too scared to have a knife anywhere near my body or face but also imagine if it went wrong and your face didn't move and you had a constant look of surprise about you—how awful!

Basically, I just need to move more and eat less which really is just common sense. I know I need to walk, run, exercise as much as possible and I do enjoy it but finding the time to do it isn't as easy as it sounds.

I have, however, developed a great love for running and think everyone should give it a go. I started running late in life, in my mid-thirties, and that was only due to my friend betting me that I couldn't run the Windsor 8K charity race with her, to which I reluctantly agreed and put in the hard hours of training as I was a novice so needed to get "running fit". A few days before the race, my friend pulled out—I was not impressed but decided not to let all that hard work go to waste so I went for it alone which was quite scary as I had never done anything like that before. What if I couldn't make it to the finish line or keeled over halfway round as the route is notoriously hilly, and with all those people watching? Terrifying! I lined up with the other runners and was so nervous I was nearly sick. The start horn blew and off we all went at a jogging pace up the 'Long Walk' which, true to its name, is a very long straight path with a dip in the middle so the true distance of it is very deceiving and then straight into a hill. Oh dear, I was puffed out after ten minutes. However, I soon settled into my own pace and ignored everyone running past me as I knew I would catch them up later (which I did!) as it was not a sprint race. Eight kilometres later and I had got round fairly easily and really, really enjoyed it. From that day on, I was hooked and I now have all the gear going: the latest in dry fit tops, proper running trainers that are really light and springy which makes it easier to bounce along, headband and gloves for winter running and a GPS watch so I know how far I have gone. It's always a nice surprise when you have gone further than you thought. All of the kit really helps when running, but you don't need all that stuff, and anyone can start as I did with an old T-shirt and pair of trainers—that's all you need and it's something you can do for the rest of your life. Even now, as a forty-something, I manage to hobble down the stairs with my bad Achilles while swinging my leg around to click my hip back into place before I start my stretches, so anyone can go out and run and it really does make you feel better when you have done it, both in mind and body—honest!

If I could go out into the park every day I would as I really do need to do a lot more exercise as I seem to have developed a 'muffin top' which I didn't notice creeping up on me until it was like a huge rubber ring around my middle and one that I seriously need to lose. How did that happen? No amount of clothing covers it up but just clings to it and hangs off it like a shelf and no clothes look nice on, which is very depressing as in my younger days I used to be able to pick anything up off the shop rail and it would fit. I have tried them all: lovely floaty summer dresses that make me look pregnant (I'm not), tight tops and jeans to try and hold it all in but it has to go somewhere and ends up bulging in all the wrong places, so leggings and flowing tops rule which I don't like wearing.

I always thought of myself growing old as an elegant and well-dressed woman—kind of like Jane Seymour or Honor Blackman—but the current reality is that if I don't stop eating so much chocolate and curb my passion for wine soon, I fear I may expand into Giant Haystacks (Google him!). Maybe even, and more seriously, I will keel over and not reach sixty which is an actual reality and slightly scary.

But, I'm not about to give everything nice up as I do like to try new things that come my way. Different foods including every new type of cheese I can get my hands on, new wines and most definitely champagnes as I am sure there is always a new grape or blend out there to be discovered and, of course, any new activity, however extreme so I can say I have done it or at least tried it.

I'm not really very good at any one thing. As the saying goes, 'Jack of all trades and master of none', but I'd rather have experienced as much as humanly possible than spend my years just focussing on one thing; not great for careers advice but good for a well-rounded person—well that's what I say anyway!

This, at least, is definitely true for sports, I'm not an expert at any one in particular but really love water sports, and waterskiing is one of my great loves. Even though I have been doing it for a number of years now, I'm still just OK and will never be Olympic standard but I have such good fun. I didn't start that until in my thirties when my step-sister introduced me to it. I used to go every weekend to the lake in Sonning where I used to sail with my dad, but I just couldn't get the hang of it for some reason so spent most of my time swimming as I constantly fell in, diving head first into the water and scooping up a load of slimy weed in my mouth. I was heading towards giving up but, being slightly stubborn, I was getting quite annoyed and frustrated with myself that I couldn't do it, but then, one day, it suddenly all clicked into place! I absolutely love it now and have my own mono ski, where you have one foot in front of the other on one ski. It's second-hand, of course as new ones are expensive, and very old-fashioned now as I think most of the modern ones are lightweight fibreglass and mine is more like a painted plank of heavy wood, but it does the job for me. There is nothing better than the feeling of going for an early morning ski in the summer when there is no wind and the water is so still it looks like a mirror with the sun glistening off it. The roar of the speedboat as its engine starts up still gives me goosebumps every time I sit in the water behind it.

My nerves kick in and my heart feels like it is going to explode out of my chest as the driver waits for me to give him the signal to, "hit it!" As my arms are yanked out of their sockets, I hang on for dear life, hoping I can make it to standing and not diving. I attempt to go around the buoys along the slalom course, however, only manage a few, then the corners test your arms as they start shaking and you fight to hold on. Coming out of the turn, you bump over the wake and your face is sprayed with water as you head back down the straight; with the sun on your face, gliding over the lake, it really is the most amazing and exhilarating feeling. The feeling the next morning is even more amazing when you wake up and can't move your arms at all as they are so painful and, on many occasions, I have had to roll myself sideways out of bed without using my arms, which is interesting! You feel as though your shoulders are ten feet wide, your legs ache and even your stomach hurts which is actually great as you really feel every part of your body is alive and you've had the most amazing workout!

I'm lucky enough to live near a few ski lakes and one of my favourite ones sits at the back of a theme park so you can hear the screams of the people on the rides while skiing. They have four massive and really beautiful lakes, three lakes for boats and one for the cable wakeboarding. There's also a bar with cool music playing so you really feel like you are on holiday. The other lake I go to has the most incredible inflatable assault course, paddle boarding and banana rides on offer, a man-made beach with sun loungers, a really fantastic clubhouse serving food and drinks and the people working there are really friendly and helpful, so why not give it a try? On a sunny day it really is the best place to be as you can spend all day there people watching or taking part in the water sports, sunbathing and listening to the music while having a coffee (or nice cold beer!). I'm sure there is a lake nearby you or, if you are really lucky and live by the sea, give it a go, if nothing else it is fresh air, exercise and a bit of fun.

Whenever I'm on holiday I have to play water polo, which I love, if a match is organised. These are only fun games with the other holidaymakers and in a normal pool with a shallow end rather than a proper water polo pool which is really deep. It's quite aggressive and, as I am short, I'm at a bit of a disadvantage when the rest of the team are sometimes six-foot-tall men. I'm constantly treading water, trying not to get pushed under, but I love to have a go anyway and I normally laugh my way through the whole match having never touched the ball and being smacked in the face and kicked a few times!

Windsurfing is not my strong point either, as I only seem to be able to go in one direction and I'm not able to turn around—not funny when you are miles away from the coast and still being blown out further. I remember I went to Lanzarote with my boyfriend, Christopher, on a windsurfing holiday. I spent most of my time swimming after my board, much to Christopher's amusement as he sailed on by waving and laughing at me as he asked what I was doing and if I was having a nice swim!

Canoeing. I first tried this on one of those outdoor activity holidays when I was very young and I remember we all had to line the canoes up and hold on to each other while we took it in turns to walk across the front of them all, and then back to our own canoe—it was really funny! I tried canoeing again a few times in my thirties and forties at local lakes and the river which is close by and also had a go a kayaking which I'm OK at and did enjoy it but generally had a constant wobble on the whole time, thinking I was going to fall in so wouldn't rush to do it again.

White-water rafting was amazing but scared me to death and I thought I was going to drown so non repeatable. More on that later...

Surfing was fantastic! I went for a long weekend with my friend, Simone, to Newquay in Cornwall as that was the 'place to surf', although I think she came reluctantly as she is not really into sports as much as me but was always up for a go at things. I was rubbish, of course, and I actually don't remember ever being able to stand up. I do remember that, as the beginner boards at that time were made of polystyrene, they soaked up the water and became extremely heavy so the next day I could hardly move having been tossed around in the waves, swimming, paddling, falling off and being hit by the board. I felt as if I had done ten rounds with Mike Tyson, however, I would definitely have another go, oddly!

Many people think that sailing is expensive to try but it is not as bad as you may think; look up your local sailing club and I am sure you can go and try it out as it is very good fun. In my twenties I booked myself on an RYA (Royal Yachting Association) weekend sailing course but I couldn't seem to get the hang of the wind directions, navigation and generally any of the written technical stuff you need to learn so I don't think I will ever be an around the world champion sailor and would always have to go with an experienced skipper, which is fine. I did once apply to sail in a leg of the Volvo Ocean Race (well, why not?) and went out on one of the amazing boats for a trial day which was incredible as those boats can sure pick up some speed! I remember when we were going at a fast rate of knots and the boat was tipped right over on one side so we all had to sit on the edge of the high side of the boat for weight distribution with our legs hanging over the edge—so exhilerating! I was also lucky that, on that particular day, the RNLI (Royal National Lifeboat Institution) did a training rescue using our boat to lower someone onto the deck from a helicopter; they are very brave and amazing people and I take my hat off to them, especially as they are mostly volunteers. However, during my trial day having seen the very confined sleeping quarters and realising that just one leg of the race was equal to about my annual salary, I didn't continue the process.

I enjoy a bit of tennis every now and then but only outside in the summer. It's not really my strong sport but it's useful to know how to play if anyone suggests doubles so I can shock them with my powerful forehand. I once had a lesson and hit the ball so hard I nearly took the coach out, much to her surprise and mine!

Squash is a really good one for getting a sweat on and quite a few gyms have squash courts. I tend to get a bit over excited and start jumping around to ensure I hit the ball. Once it ended in disaster as I landed on my turned in foot making me think I had broken it and I was embarrassingly lying on the floor of the squash court crying with a massive swollen and purple ankle for everyone to see. I haven't played since and will never play again but at least I have had a go.

I've tried quite a few things and I basically have to say 'yes' if someone offers me the opportunity to try something that I haven't yet done. So, any ideas of new activities or even amazing places to visit for a day out, please let me know; as long as it doesn't involve heights!

So, as far as a dream life is concerned, I'm not sure if I would call it quite that, but all in all, I think I've had an all-round average life so far, with more to strive for but I do consider myself lucky that I have had so many

amazing   opportunities   and   experiences   already
compared to some.

Those precious and great years from my late teens
to my thirties definitely shaped me and how my life and
outlook are today.

Chapter Two
France

My sister and her husband decided to buy a little house in northern France so they could go over for holidays and eventually retire over there. The house was, as per their main house in England, virtually derelict when they bought it, so they got it for a really good price. It is quite remote with only two other houses nearby and really quiet with only the sound of cockerels to break the silence. You have to get in the car to go to the local shops, which are situated in a quaint town where everything is centered around a church sat right in the middle. It has the typically French *boulangerie* that sells the most amazing bread and cakes, a pub, supermarket and a stunning flower shop, plus there is a large fishing lake nearby where Arnold loves to spend an afternoon. What more could you need!

Of course, my sister managed to buy the house from a man who, not long after, was to appear on the TV as a wanted man having been exposed as a rogue trader. My sister is not one to let people walk all over her and, even though this man had disappeared off the face of the earth whilst in the middle of renovating her house, she managed to hunt him down and make him finish all the work he promised to do and that she had paid him for. She can be quite scary at times!

So, the plan was for me to go to France with Jane and Arnold as soon as possible after they first bought the house: an experience that will stay with me forever. We are so different in many ways; she likes Glastonbury mud, wellies and camping and I like a warm clean comfortable bed, my slippers and a hairdryer.

I was quite excited going over to see their new home and had high expectations for the house just like you see in *Escape to the Country*, a quaint property built with local stone, blue shutters with beautiful flowers around them and a decked area at the back overlooking fields to enjoy the long warm evenings while drinking *vin rouge* and eating a baguette filled with creamy *fromage* and only the sound of crickets to be heard, aaaahhhhh, heavenly.

But no. Not my sister's style. As we flew into the airport, the torrential rain lashed the plane and the gale force winds blew us sideways, which wasn't the best start. We picked up the hire car and it took most of the journey to the house for my sister to get to grips with driving on the other side of the road, squealing round the hairpin bends on two wheels in the pouring rain, so my nerves were already in tatters and I was looking forward to a nice hot cup of coffee in comfort. We finally arrived at dusk, a few hours later than planned following a few wrong turns but I was just relieved to be there in one piece having been scared to death for the whole journey. Now we could start our holiday.

I like to look nice when I travel so had put on a nice skirt and high heels as I knew we weren't walking far. As the rain poured down, I rushed to get out of the car and head for shelter in the house, but as I jumped out of the car and my feet touched the ground, I started to sink... and sink... and sink. It was like quicksand but muddier. In fact, it was like a quagmire. My eyes slowly adjusted to the fading light, as we were in the middle of nowhere there were no street lights, so the only light was from the moon but as it was covered by the black clouds, I couldn't see a thing. I realised I was standing in the middle of a football pitch-sized mud bath, in the pouring rain, freezing cold and in my stilettos. Oh well, I thought, let's get inside and we can dry off and warm up in front of the log fire with a nice *vin rouge*. You think I would have been getting the picture by this stage, but I think I am naturally an optimist which, in this instance, may have been rather naive. I was heading towards the house when my sister yelled at me, "This way", and pointed in the other direction. We headed towards a cowshed-type building which was one of their outbuildings. That was to be our accommodation for the night. It turned out that the main house was uninhabitable at this point so we had to stay in the smaller annex with its outside toilet that had no light, a muddy floor and freezing cold, thick concrete walls. They were absolutely covered in cobwebs, which made my imagination run wild with thoughts of giant spiders coming to get me during the night, entangling me into their web before slowly devouring me for breakfast. Deep joy. I tried to not drink anything to avoid having to use it.

The night went downhill from there as the discussion turned to the sleeping arrangements as it was late and we were all very tired. A bed was supposed to have been delivered that day, however, of course the rogue trader who my sister had enlisted to carry out this task hadn't kept to his word so nothing had arrived. Unfortunately, this meant that all three of us had to share a bed in a damp room with one electric heater for warmth. Whatever vision has sprung into your mind, it is completely wrong, and some of you may think that Arnold's eyes would have lit up at this prospect and he would have enjoyed this, however, you couldn't be further from the truth. As my sister is very tall and likes her space, she took one side of the bed and I took the other side, leaving poor Arnold sandwiched in the middle. We all had four layers of clothes, including four pairs of socks as it was so cold, so poor Arnold was not left which much space. Well, at least we had a bed. It's amazing how quickly your standards drop and you get used to the bare essentials so I thought if I could just get to sleep quickly it would be morning before we knew it and we could sort out the new beds. I shivered myself to sleep, only to be woken up half an hour later wondering what I could feel on my face. Maybe it was

Arnold's hair or just the covers which were pulled right up as I was trying to keep my nose warm. Arnold then woke up and said he could feel something on his leg. Oh, my goodness, it was my worst nightmare—there was an ants' nest in the old mattress! I leapt out of bed and threw the covers back to find not a few stray ants but a swarm in the bed that made me feel ill and itch all over. Arnold very kindly swept the ants away and we tried to settle down on the top of the duvet in the hope the ants wouldn't get us. My sister snored her way through the whole incident and, in the morning, woke up refreshed to a very grumpy sister (me) and husband both looking as though we hadn't slept for a month. Who needs to get paid a fortune to go into the jungle and be on the TV when I can do it for free? Unfortunately, when I yelled the words "I'm a Celebrity Get Me Out of Here" I just got an elbow in the ribs and told to shut up.

I can laugh about it now, but only just and think the experience has scarred me for life. However, I have been back since, to much improvement, but I still secretly cringe slightly when greeted with the dead mice on the bed that need disposing of each time they go over there but that is rural living for you

My sister and Arnold have both spent a lot more time doing up the house which looks amazing from the photos I've seen and I am sure I will return again when I am feeling braver, but definitely not in the winter and

I will definitely be wearing wellies instead of stilettos, whatever the weather.

Arnold is lovely and makes us all laugh. He sometimes walks round in just a paint-covered sweatshirt, his socks and baggy old underpants that have turned grey in the wash, with a roll-up cigarette hanging out of his mouth, holding a can of weak beer as he doesn't like the strong stuff. He is a painter and decorator and a very good one at that as he is very particular about getting things just right and is immaculately tidy. His very thick head of hair is always coated in dried paint and he is one of the nicest blokes you will ever meet with a very good, but dry, sense of humour. He's incredibly knowledgeable, intelligent and wise, so never fails to surprise me with various historical and geographical facts and figures that he randomly comes out with.

This photo of them on holiday makes me laugh whenever I see it as it sums up my sister and Arnold and teaches me to not take things too seriously, laugh at myself and enjoy every new experience I have.

Chapter Three
The real travel bug

I think I have a pretty 'average' life compared to others. I have to go to work, as most people do, to pay the mortgage and bills and really don't like my job as many people don't. That Sunday night feeling of dread and depression knowing you have a full week ahead, the feeling getting worse during winter as I struggle to get up in the mornings when it is dark and cold and the feeling I should be hibernating or, even better, on a beach somewhere, really sets in. I dream about winning the lottery as I'm sure everyone does, especially when times are tough, and I know I spend way too much on tickets that I never win anything on. I certainly won't be adding up the amount I have spent as I'm sure it would be quite shocking.

So real life for me is working as a corporate event manager, arranging conferences and events around the world, which is where I think my travel bug started. I realised that not only could I experience countries that I would never normally go to but, I could be paid to go and do something that I really enjoyed at the same time—what could be better!

Unfortunately, now, after over twenty years in this industry, things have changed and the pace and demanding nature of the work has increased twofold. It now entails too much constant travelling, too much stress, too many hours sitting on my bum in the office with steam coming off the keyboard only looking up twice a day from multiple online meetings and then way too many early mornings and late nights. In my twenties and thirties, I used to love it; the excitement of putting together an event abroad, going to new places and that proud feeling as I watched an event take place that I had played a part in organising.

Those were the days where budgets were huge and money was spent on lavish parties and product launches, cars to pick me up and business class seats on the plane, the best hotels and restaurants and hardly ever a late night in the office. However, the good old days are no longer with us and, with budgets cut right back to the bone, many of the exciting events have all but disappeared as we get squashed into economy seats on long-haul flights and stuck in box-like hotel rooms and then having to get up at four thirty each morning. Definitely not glamorous any more, or maybe I have just got old and like my creature comforts and sleep!

Oh no, I have turned into a grumpy old woman!

However, I don't want to put anyone off, really, as it has been great for the last twenty years and I wouldn't change it for the world. So if you or your kids are looking for a career with some excitement then I would definitely recommend going down this path as there are still some really great companies out there who you can travel the world with while arranging the most spectacular events, seeing some amazing countries, meeting really interesting people who you wouldn't normally come into contact within a 'normal' job and really progress your career if you are willing to work hard, so the world really is your oyster.

I've been really lucky in visiting so many countries through work and, although the schedule is normally very full on with minimal time for sleeping, I always manage to squeeze in a few hours to see something of the place I'm in—otherwise there really wouldn't be much point.

I've eaten in a very upmarket restaurant overlooking the iconic glass pyramid of the Louvre in Paris, driven motorised beer kegs around an army base in Germany, strolled around the back streets of Boston during Halloween enjoying all the elaborately dressed doorsteps with carved pumpkins, candles and cobwebs, followed by eating the best surf and turf I've ever had at Ruth's & Chris's. I've sailed on a Global Challenge yacht, stayed in a plush hotel overlooking lake Luzern, hosted a group at Chelsea Flower Show, sampled a few Guinesses in Dublin, visited the Little Mermaid in Copenhagen and explored the canals and nightlife of both Amsterdam and Birmingham! But I'm not boasting or being smug as I know I have just been really, really lucky.

I know Barcelona and Cannes like the back of my hand and love them both, however, I have also worked seventeen-hour days in a conference centre with no windows, had a toenail fall off due to pounding concrete conference floors for a couple of weeks, and been abroad to just see a hotel room and the venue and nothing else whatsoever. So swings and roundabouts but it's definitely more of a lifestyle choice and the good really does outweigh the bad.

A few of my favourite events in Switzerland were back in those good old days. Everything was so much easier and less stressful back then as these events were all just small meetings but, due to the status of the attendees, I needed to go along to ensure everything ran smoothly. As the event co-ordinator, along with some very clever but very technical colleagues, otherwise referred to as 'geeks' who I got on with like a house on fire, I went to these meetings where really all I had to do was ensure the meeting space was setup, coffee and lunch were served on time, retrieve the boxes of collateral I had sent and ensure travel and accommodation was OK: so really easy and lovely jobs.

We stayed in the most beautiful hotels that I would never ordinarily be able to afford, plus we had free time in the evenings to explore the city and, as expenses were not tight in those days, I remember in Zurich we went to some amazing restaurants located down old cobbled streets and on the edge of the lake, that I would never have found or gone to if I were just on holiday. I think this was when travelling was really exciting and my love of Europe started, especially Switzerland, France and southern Germany as I was finding magical places off the beaten track that many people have never experienced. I would still love to discover more of these hidden gems that stay in your memory for ever.

Unfortunately, these types of jobs are long gone and really don't exist any more which is a sign of the times but still a great shame.

One of the more challenging events I have worked on (to put it mildly), was a job in New York working for a large event agency in the UK whose client was a well-known electronics company that are notoriously challenging to work for.

I don't know how the girl running the project for the client didn't have a nervous breakdown as the core team had been working on this for months prior to me joining so were stressed an exhausted already. Thankfully I was only managing one hundred and twenty hosts/hostesses and brand ambassadors. Well, I say 'only', my three weeks in the office prior to going on site were very stressful with long hours, often not leaving the office until gone ten p.m. having had no dinner and then still an hour's commute home, although some of the girls pulled all nighters which I think is totally out of order and shrinks your day rate to below the minimum wage! This is when the event weight gain starts as you are eating at silly times and there would often be cake and sweets in the office to cheer everyone up and, when you are tired, your will power is non existent.

The ladies running this project were the most experienced, and all of us older and more "hardy" freelancers were brought in due to the client's reputation of being tough to work for. On this occasion they unbelieveably managed to surpass this, often changing their mind at the last minute, causing work that had taken weeks to plan to then be re-done very quickly, and expecting us to work twenty-four hours a day.

My dad still doesn't really quite understand what I actually do at work as many people don't and the first question I normally get asked is, "Oh do you arrange weddings?" Which I don't. To be fair, it is actually quite difficult to explain depending on what I'm looking after on each event; whether it is crew (which on one event was over five hundred people), security, food and beverage or hosts/hostesseswhich are all really detailed pieces of work when the event is for ten thousand or more delegates, or if a smaller event I would run the whole thing, but each with its own tight budget to be carefully managed.

For this particular job I needed to get uniforms for one hundred and twenty men and women in exactly the same outfits at the cheapest price possible. You would think that is an easy task, however, when you get into actually trying to find those numbers of very specific shirts, trousers and shoes for sizes ranging from size zero to a size twenty, you can only order certain amounts of each online and then sizes run out. You then have to order from US and European websites, ensuring the sizing was correct, plus the company credit card was often stopped due to potential fraudulence, it was a bit of a challenge.

I created a detailed day by day, hour by hour schedule for the hosts and hostesses so they even knew when they could go to the toilet, along with a detailed briefing document and presentation that I was to deliver on site, plus booked all the crew flights which, again, is not a straightforward task. I ensured lockers were the right size for the one hundred and twenty staff, orderd the crew badges and lanyards (the rope bit that goes around your neck), of course with the correct pantone reference and branding, carefully working within the budget, and helped out some of the others who were seriously overloaded; so three weeks actually wasn't very long at all.

So, having worked long hours in the office and already flagging, we then flew to New York for a gruelling twelve days to build and prepare for the three events we were doing. We arrived at what is apparently an upmarket and very trendy central New York hotel to find that, in my case, the room was so small I had to do a three-point turn with my bag to even get it in the door. You had to walk past the bed sideways to get to the bathroom and heaven knows why they put a door on the bathroom as there is no way it could have been closed. The blackout blind on the window was broken so I held it up with the 'trash can' for the duration of my stay as the hotel didn't seem to be able to fix it. Due to luck of the draw, my room was one of the bigger ones...

After checking in, it was straight to work for the first late night on site which felt even worse due to travelling and jet lag plus the enormous burger and fries I decided to eat, not realising how large the portions were over there and getting totally over excited at the amount of chips I got, so obviously eating them all making me feel even more sluggish. Finally, we got to go to bed, so as I usually do, I tried to open the windows for some fresh air, to find that they were welded shut and so didn't open. I reluctantly put the air conditioning on which was so noisy and sounded, as my colleague put it, "Like someone was throwing spanners at the windows", and then came the very long process of trying to work out how to turn off all the various lights in the room with numerous switches. With all of that it is not surprising that I didn't get much sleep.

I was up early the next day as, on site days, you always start around seven a.m. for the morning meeting so hairwash, breakfast and start the walk to the venue all before six thirty a.m. and with jet lag I had absolutely no idea what the time was. This continued for the twelve days, often not leaving the venue or eating until eleven p.m. but each night waking up at two a.m. feeling starving to which M&Ms were usually a quick fix—all adding to the on site weight gain.

The amount of pavement pounding to and from the venue and constantly around the venue on concrete floors took its toll on all of our feet—black toenails, swollen and painful ankles and feet and one girl even got trench foot! It was tough going.

The team were unbelievably tired, getting irritable with their own colleagues and friends within their own smaller teams such as Production or IT. Breaking out in spots and rashes, often sculking off to the toilets for a quick cry, and most vowed never to work on the event again for which I don't blame them, and that also included me.

Luckily for me however, my logistics team mates all knew each other very well and we all got on, so even when things were really tough on site, we never had a problem and actually the opposite applied as we all got a bit giddy and were laughing hysterically at certain points throught the day much to everyone else's annoyance I think.

One of the girls who was a friend of a friend on the job and who I hadn't worked with before, turned out to be my personal comedian on site – quite apt really as she actually worked as a comedian in her spare time. She was so funny and often came out with one liners, that had me crying with laughter while sat at my computer in our makeshift office.

One of the comments she made virtually every time she saw me, was to ask me what channel I had my radio on and if I was on the correct group to which I would say that of course I was. She would then hear the robotic voice on the radios being switched around—five, four, three, two, as I was secretly checking and switching channels to make sure I was. I'm sure she did this on purpose every day just for a laugh… and I think you had to be there, but it was the funniest thing.

One of the stranger things, that by the end of the twelve days had become an annoyance, was the fact that everywhere was so dark. In the hotel you had to watch carefully where you were walking as you couldn't see any steps, and in the lift (or elevator as it is called in the US), the buttons for the floors were so dark you couldn't read them so had to memorise where your floor button was located to feel your way along—almost like Braille. In every restaurant we would look around to see that all the other customers at the tables had their phone torches out to read the menus—I'm sure it is supposed to be atmospheric but taken to the extreme and truly ridiculous!

Another surreal time during this job which I can laugh at now but at the time my friend and I had a serious sense of humour failure, was on a Sunday night when the client decided they wanted three hundred different coloured tops for some of the hosts/brand ambassadors to wear, and they wanted them immediately. Of course.

Due to the volume of tops required and deadline for deliveries on a Sunday, I tried without success to get them online, so my friend and I were sent over to New Jersey in a taxi to a well known store in the USA on a Sunday night at ten p.m. It was quite ridiculous walking round with two trollies stacked full of as many tops as we could get, clearing rails until they were bare and still not managing to get the full three hundred.

The man on the checkout was not best pleased and told us he was supposed to be finishing his shift within the next five minutes, which of course didn't happen.

With our English accents, my friend and I stuck out like a sore thumb and having paid for all our goods and carrying dozens of bags, soon realised, while standing in the car park of this store at midnight in the pouring rain, trying to get a cab back, that this really wasn't the place to be. The last straw was when a very large truck with blacked out windows started cruising the car park, driving round and round with a large flagpole welded on the back of the truck and a picture of a black eagle flying in the wind. Very scary. Two men then approached us and offered us a lift as it was clear we couldn't get a cab, and thought we would actually like to get in the car with them... REALLY!

Very luckily, my friend had an Uber account on her phone which came to our rescue; well, the driver was weird but at least we were on our way back. Phew.

I compare that evening and the clientele of that particular shop to the film *Deliverence* which I purchased on DVD and watched in the comfort of my own home when I returned, thanking my lucky stars that we had both survived unscathed.

Some of the girls stayed on a few days after the event but New York is so expensive—even the one-day extra that I stayed cost more than a day's pay, so all in all not a great job although the camaraderie was brilliant.

Finally, I was on the plane home! Thank goodness. I breathed a sigh of relief until I realised that I had seven hours sat next to a lady that smelt of wee.

If that doesn't put you off, then go for it!

After that event I felt as though I had done my travelling, well most of it, and thought that I would like to do something a bit more worthwhile—get involved in actual real-world issues that are important and actually affect people's lives. Spend time with old people to try and make their day more interesting, help animals or protect trees—just something to make a real difference to someone else—I guess it's called 'giving something back'. Such a cliché but I think as you get older you really do feel that way. But I also want to make lots of money and the two don't generally go together...

Chapter Four
My mad twenties

I think my twenties were the years that really shaped my life as I had a ton of energy, as you do at that age, and not much responsibility, so I packed my time with a huge amount of life changing experiences, going everywhere, trying everything and generally living life at a hundred miles an hour. I also think that my very loving and stable upbringing gave me the confidence and support to do this, which I will be eternally grateful for.

Having left school with not many qualifications to my name and just a one-year college course in office studies, I have been very lucky with the jobs I have managed to get. The booming eighties were an amazing time with an endless supply of jobs to pick and choose from with a virtual guarantee that you would get anything you applied for, so I consider myself lucky to have been starting out at that time.

My lack of qualifications, were not because I didn't pay attention at school, quite the opposite really as I have always liked to learn so did do my best to take things in. However, my mind does tend to wander rather easily, and a very short concentration span still affects me today, but I was very well behaved, never got into any trouble and tried my best at all subjects. I was pleasantly surprised when I was moved up a class in biology, disappointed when I was moved down a class in physics as I loved it but, as I was rubbish at maths, I wasn't allowed to continue. I was, however, really good at English if I do say so myself, although since the introduction of 'spell check' my spelling has deteriorated a tad, and I even got a qualification in motor mechanics with the exam practical being to put a motorbike back together from scratch. I'm not quite sure how I managed it and do remember that I hid some of the bits I didn't know what to do with and even tied some on with wire so at least they looked as though they were in the right place. Being given the option, I decided that motor mechanics and metalwork were far more interesting than the alternative of sewing. In hindsight, sewing would have been more useful but I guess as long as I can sew on a button (which I can if I have to) and have my best friend Wonder Web to shorten trousers which I have to do on virtually every pair, then everything is OK as far as I'm concerned. As for motor mechanics, I don't have much use for building motorbikes and would call roadside assistance should my wheel need changing but I can detect a squeaking fan belt and check my oil and coolant levels, plus it was great fun at the time. I wanted to take French but was put in a German class which I now actually think is easier to learn than French, however, I don't remember much from those lessons which is a real shame and something I regret not concentrating on more.

My very first job after college was at a big IT corporation, working on reception and sorting the mail. It paid about four thousand pounds a year which seemed like a lot of money at the time but, more importantly, it was the first rung on the ladder to corporate life and the beginning of years of fun. Yes, working can actually be fun if you are in the right job with good people around you!

I worked my way up to a secretarial position as I had my typing skills from college—I knew it would come in handy—and then embarked on my many years of temping, working at various companies moving around all of the departments and getting to know absolutely everyone which, as an enthusiastic and sociable twenty-something, was amazing.

Those were the days. Not a care in the world, living at home, paying a very small amount of rent and always having spare cash in my pocket to go out and enjoy myself.

As work was in abundance, I carried on temping in secretarial jobs for years until the seven-year itch kicked in and I decided it was time to move on. I got a lovely job organising training courses where I had to travel to London a couple of times a week which was fantastic and really exciting at the time. All the trainers were really nice and we used to go out for drinks after work every week without fail which I used to look forward to.

I thought this was the best thing ever as we mingled in the bars with all the city workers in their smart suits. Oh, nothing beats the bright lights of London when you are young!

I was at the company, for a good few years, and during this time, I was at the age where I wanted to spread my wings so decided to move out of home into the big scary world to stand on my own two feet. I wasn't sure where to live but wanted somewhere with a bit more life on the doorstep so, while in the pub one Friday lunchtime, I took a map with me, closed my eyes and put a pin in it! The nearest town to my pin was Windsor so that's where I decided to go which I am very pleased about now, as some of the other places on the map could have led to a very different outcome! I had been to Windsor before and always loved it as, every time I went, it felt like I was on holiday with the river, the boats, the many tourists from all over the world and the cafe culture with its great atmosphere.

I found a room for rent, one of five rooms in a very large house in the middle of Windsor with a lovely walled garden and it didn't take me long to settle in. Luckily, my housemates were great fun so we would all go out together in Windsor as we were so close to the action or, if anyone was short of money, we used to invite friends around to the house for garden parties, which were often quite a boozy affair!

I was having a great time both at home and at work but was always looking for more excitement, so when on a normal day at work, a colleague of mine was talking about her days as a holiday rep and all the fun times she had. This, of course, planted the seed in my head and was the inevitable next move for me; as if by magic an advert appeared in the paper for a well-known holiday company looking for new reps—it must have been fate! I got in touch with them and went to London for the interview which I have to say was quite nerve-racking as I had to stand up and do a presentation as though I was holding a welcome meeting in resort. I was allowed to choose my own subject, but it had to be funny, interesting and bold as I was presenting to my fellow applicants so it had to beat the competition.

Amazingly, I got the job and things went from being just fun, to being mad fun.

Chapter Five
The Algarve, Portugal

I think that everyone should have a go at being a holiday rep or something similar. It really did change my life and my whole outlook on things plus my horizons were definitely broadened—all in a positive way.

I was very lucky to get the holiday rep job and I still think it was one of my 'braver' decisions as, at twenty-six, I was one of the older reps and had no experience. But really—how difficult could it be?!

I flew alone, sitting on the plane full of nerves, wondering what on earth I had done. When I arrived at Faro airport, I was met by the head rep who seemed very friendly and pleased to see me, which was a good start. She had her own car so we set off to where I was going to be staying, however, by this time it was starting to get dark so I couldn't really tell where we were headed for and I tried to work it out by looking at the intermittent road signs which didn't help in the slightest as they were in Portuguese. We finally reached our destination and I was dropped off in the 'Old Town Algarve'. Having passed a few lovely looking hotels, hoping that each was going to be my new home for the summer, I suddenly found myself on my own, in a dingy apartment with a bathroom shared by lots of old men. The mould around the bath and the obvious smell of a toilet occupied by lots of men (sorry to generalise) was awful. Oh, my goodness—I was horrified. What on earth did I think I was doing and what did the company think they were doing by housing me there? If I could have contacted anyone, I think I would have gone straight back to the airport and flown home that night but, as I was totally alone with no phone numbers for anyone and hardly any money, I had to stay the night. Needless to say, I didn't get much sleep as I spent the whole night planning my excuse to leave or what felt like escape, first thing the next morning.

As the sun came up, I realised that I had been put in the old fogey part of town with all the OAP holidaymakers, no clubs and certainly no young people. Really, it is saying something when a twenty-six-year-old is considered as past it.

It took me a few days to take it all in, get my bearings and get used to my surroundings. What should I do—stay or go? Right, I thought to myself, I'm not giving up that easily and really have to stay more than a few days to give it a go and see what happens. So, give it a go I did which was the best decision I ever made.

The Algarve in southern Portugal is such a beautiful place and my memories of it will stay with me forever. The beaches are amazing—long stretches of golden sand with a rugged coastline, piercing blue water and always a deep blue sky.

I had some time to wander round the town to locate the hotels I would be looking after. The 'Old Town Algarve' was a working fishing village; the local brightly coloured blue, red and yellow fishing boats were perched on the sand and, in the afternoons, the fishermen would sit mending their vast nets ready for the next early morning fishing trip.

My apartment was at the top of a hill and on the main path leading into the town. As I walked down the cobbled streets towards the centre, I was hit by a mouth-watering smell of barbequing sardines and garlic wafting around me making me instantly hungry. All the streets led into a main town square and it had such a friendly feel. It was one of those places that make you feel at home and like you belong there. Everywhere I turned there were hidden alleyways lined with whitewashed buildings covered in bright pink flowers and lovely old lanterns leading the way down to the picturesque golden sandy beach and the glistening sea beyond: I fell in love with it.

Being a rep, of course, I had to wear a uniform. I'm not sure who designed them but they had obviously never been to Portugal in the summer as the suits were made of wool which was totally impractical in forty-degree heat and we were told that we were not allowed to take our jackets off. Unfortunately, to add to this, because I was one of the later arriving reps, I was left with the uniform sizes that no one else wanted, massive sack like shirts made of polyester that drowned me and a skirt that had to be held up with a very tightly pulled in belt or it would fall off. The jacket was so massive I could have worn it on its own as a dress and, at that time, shoulder pads were all the rage but they made me look like I was five feet wide—ridiculous!

I do have to admit that the first couple of months were very tough as I was quite isolated from the other reps, so I made it my mission to get to know all the locals on my 'patch' and for them to all know me. After a few weeks, my persistence had paid off and I knew everyone; all the restaurant, hotel and bar owners, and I came to love walking around the town saying hello to everyone and having people wave at me when I went past. I was so pleased that I was here with the beach so close, traditional restaurants and live music in the bars—far away from the pumping disco strip and drunken teenagers—I was actually very lucky and had been placed in the very best location and take back what I said about it being for OAPs! A lesson to always give things a chance and never judge too quickly.

All the reps from the other resorts met up once a week for the company meeting which was a bit daunting being both the older one and the new one. However, I got really friendly with two of the other reps while I was there who were based in the next resort and luckily had cars. I am still in touch with one of them but unfortunately lost touch with the other a few years ago. I would really like to find her again so hopefully she will read this and make contact. Amanda was the first girl I became friendly with as we liked to do the same things on our day off, unlike the other reps who would be out drinking all night and in bed with a hangover for the whole next day which I thought was a complete waste of a day off. We liked to get out and about, have an adventure and go sightseeing and, of course, a bit of sunbathing. Naturally we always had a few drinks along the way but wanted to actually see and experience the culture and the country.

Oh, I can't tell you how much fun Amanda and I had. She was a tall, thin girl with short blonde curly hair just like Marilyn Monroe and she always wore bright red lipstick. She had a really strong northern accent with a sense of humour to match, which was absolutely brilliant. In spite of her height, she always wore high heels and I remember one pair were kind of wedge-like but wooden which sounds very strange but they were amazing. However, they were totally impractical on the unmade and potholed roads much to Amanda's detrement as, on the eve of our day off, she went over on her ankle down a kerb—ouch —but she didn't want to miss out on a night of fun so carried on and hobbled to the bar who supplied her with a mound of ice for the very large swelling. After a few drinks she didn't feel it so had a great night until the next morning when the pain set in! Her apartment was really nice, light and airy with modern tiles and very clean. It was much better than mine, so I often stayed with her, much of the time sleeping on a mattress on the balcony as it was so hot and there was no air con which was wonderful as the sound of the crickets sent me to sleep. Just over the road and hidden away in a corner of a small outdoor shopping centre, there was a really great bar which was very handy. Well, I say great. It was a funny old place, small and very dark, in fact a bit dingy with a seventies patterned carpet that you stuck to when you walked in and you could smell the stale beer from the night before, but the people who ran it were English and from up north so we always got a true northern warm welcome, and they were all so hilarious that we all became good friends.

We spent a lot of time there, too much in fact, but it was so funny every time we went there with endless entertainment games and quizzes—all the rage in those days. We had a go at everything: sumo wrestling wearing big bouncy costumes and bungee running on an inflatable track that you always got whiplash from as the bungee snapped you back when you tried to run to the end. The *Macarena* was a weekly highlight, all stood in a row and everyone knowing all the dance moves. All extremely cheesy but our sides ached from laughing so much every night.

We didn't often go clubbing as the big clubs were too far to travel to, however, when we saw the new 'in thing' advertised we just had to go: FOAM PARTY! Now that did sound like fun! Off we trotted and counted out our Escudos (no Euros in those days) to get a taxi. When we arrived, we couldn't believe our eyes. We walked into the club—it was like a massive bubble bath—fantastic! There were hundreds of people crammed in, all soaking wet and very drunk! Our clothes got ruined from the foam and water but we didn't care as we had consumed quite a few strangely coloured drinks and were rather merry, to put it mildly, but we had a great time. It turned out that we knew the DJ who often worked in the funny pub near the apartment, so we got all our favourite music played and went from hysterical laughing and sliding around the floor, with me being short, desperately trying to keep my head above the foam so I wouldn't drown. Amanda was tall so didn't have the same problem but was adding to my laughter by smothering me in foam, most of which went in my mouth and up my nose. Being short is a severe disadvantage at a foam party as heels are not an option and flip flops are the obvious footwear choice. Amanda decided to 'foam me' one last time before we left and so bent down to pick up a big armful of bubbles. This was the moment that it all went pear-shaped as one of us—probably me—must have staggered forward. On her journey up from scooping bubbles from the floor her head collided with the underside of my jaw, and smashed my teeth together.

At that point, we left but, due to the anaesthetic effect of the alcohol, I didn't realise the full extent of the damage until the next morning when I had to make an emergency appointment with the dentist. Three broken teeth; it was awful and painful.

This was one of the times I actually did contemplate going home as, being on my own, I was feeling quite sorry for myself. The thought of having all that dental work done with an unknown dentist and that I may lose my front tooth was very disturbing. I called my dad and told him half the story as I didn't want him to worry too much, but just wanted to hear a friendly voice. During the conversation, and probably as I mentioned I may like to come home, I discovered that my dad's brother had made a bet with my dad that I would not last the season—how arrogant of him! Like a red rag to a bull, I braved the dentist, dug my heels in and stayed. I was certainly not going to let my uncle win the bet over my dad even if I did have to have a few false teeth.

I have a lasting reminder of that night in the form of a large crack in my front tooth but, luckily, it is still my own, and two crowns on others. Well, you need a few war wounds as they tell the story of your life and it was great fun, so I definitely have no regrets!

Of course I wasn't allowed any time off so straight back to the job in hand and, as I'm sure you all know, when you go on a package holiday, the reps will try and sell you an excursion or two. Part of our job was to talk about the trips which we would then make commission from. I was actually a very conscientious rep and only offered the trips that I thought were actually worth doing, so I was never going to make any serious money but genuinely wanted people to have a good time; to my detriment as I was always broke. To enable us to sell these effectively, we needed to go on the trips ourselves and try out all the activities so we could talk knowledgably about them. One of these was a day driving racing cars—what fun I thought! Here we go again.

Amanda and I legged it over to the race cars and bagsied the only two-seater one as I was a bit of a woose and didn't want to drive myself. As we set off in a timed race with all the other reps, losing was not an option. We whizzed around the very bendy track and, in between my hysterical laughter, I was screaming at Amanda—who was driving like a looney—to put her foot down and go faster; to which she obliged. As we sped up, we came hurtling up to a bend which we couldn't quite make, ending up driving straight into a brick wall. This time it was more serious than cracked teeth, and I think I actually lost a few minutes. I just remember sitting in the car not knowing quite what had happened and staring at Amanda's leg which had a large metal pole sticking out of it, although I had no idea what it was, where it had come from or how it had got jammed into her leg. We were taken out of the cars and, quite quickly I realised that I had done some damage to my ankle. Amanda had broken her arm plus had a massive hole in her leg from the metal pole. Thank heavens for seat belts and crash helmets: a lesson to us all. I've never actually told my dad about that as I didn't want him to worry at the time—sorry Dad.

Amanda's season was over and I was to lose a good friend for the rest of the summer. She was so upset at having to go home, and it was really sad to say goodbye.

I was oddly resilient at that age and soon got back on my feet and back to normal without any fuss or moping around but just a bit of hobbling. The holiday company wasted no time in getting a replacement for Amanda, although I have to say I was a bit worried about who would be coming. But I was introduced to Heidi. Oh, my goodness—what brilliant luck—Heidi's infectious laugh kicked in and I soon found out that she was madder than Amanda and also liked doing the same things as me. I couldn't have wished for anyone better and we got on like a house on fire. Let the shenanigans continue!

Heidi was only slightly taller than me, quite sporty and slim with brown hair but the best thing was that she was always laughing. She found the funny side of absolutely everything which I think is an amazing quality.

Heidi and I were given a company car to share, although she kept it at her place which was Amanda's old apartment. Heidi used to drop me off at my hotels and pick me up at the end of our shift, so we used to take it in turns driving. Unbelievably, this was my first time driving abroad and I have to say that Heidi was very brave in offering to teach me. As I drove down the road, I frequently kerbed the wheels, almost taking out a few pedestrians en route but soon got the hang of it, although

I was never really that keen on driving. On our regular journey between each of our hotels there was, of course, a great bar. It was a Dutch bar and restaurant where we made regular pit stops as they served really good coffee. It was called the Hoff van Holland from which came the daily phrase of 'stopping in the Hoffee for a coffee'. We were always guaranteed a very good reception from the Dutch husband and wife owners and, as usual, whenever we went, a ridiculous amount of laughing took place. They made the best sangria I have ever tasted in my life which I still stand by today, however, goodness knows what was in it but I would imagine a bit more than red wine and fruit.

Heidi and I became friendly with the guys running the bar—one Dutch and one American/Portuguese who were as mad and cheekily behaved as us—in a good way of course. We would go there and have dinner, prop up the bar while they were working and then all go out together.

One particular evening while we were having dinner, we noticed that a car outside was driving rather fast up and down the road, tyres squealing and smoking from doing wheel spins and doughnuts in the middle of the main road. We started to get annoyed and were moaning at whoever was driving, saying how bad it was and how disgusted we were with the drunken tourists that were acting like this. It took us a while, but we soon realised that our car keys were missing from the bar top. One of the boys had stolen them; it was our company car leaving its rubber on the road and attracting the attention of every passer-by and, if it had gone on for much longer, it would probably have alerted the police too who you didn't want to mess with over there. Everyone in the bar was in on it; the owners and even the customers had all been waiting for us to notice and instantly fell about laughing when we finally cottoned on, which I have to say took a while as we were enjoying our food so much! The look on our faces must have been a picture as horror set in and then panic that they would trash the car. The boys drove the car back into the car park, however, continued being naughty by driving around with one of them sat on the roof trying to drink a pint of beer, spilling most of it down the front of the car; the windscreen wipers were on full speed to clear the view. The windscreen was sticky for ages and so many flies got stuck on it we had to wash it! I'm sure some of you are horrified reading this but things were different in those days, especially abroad, and I'm sure that no one would ever dream of doing anything like that now—but at the time it was very funny.

I have to say that Heidi was occasionally a bit scatty. She once locked herself out of her apartment although I'm still not sure how, as her keys just wouldn't work. It was an unusual night and one of many I guess, but this was different. There was a storm brewing and the rain was torrential. The type that drenches you within seconds and makes you feel like you have been in a swimming pool with all your clothes on. Having stood outside for way too long getting soaked and weighing up our options on how to get back in the apartment, it turned out that we didn't actually have any options and the only thing we could do was to try and borrow a ladder to get to the upstairs window that she had left open. I'm not sure who in this town we knew would have a ladder as it was not like your normal neighbourhood. We ended up walking miles and miles to visit all the people we knew to find a ladder; still in the pouring rain and by this time pitch dark. Amazingly we managed to track down someone who had one. Heidi and I started to walk back to her apartment, both with the end of a twelve-foot ladder on our shoulders. We must have been a very odd sight and looked as though we were up to something underhand so we were lucky no one called the *Polizia* as it could have been an even more interesting night! So forget health and safety, we got to Heidi's apartment and propped the ladder up against the apartment block and climbed up it, wobbling as we went and occasionally slipping off as it was so wet and, of course, we'd had a few pit stops en route to make the best of a bad situation and drunk a few sangrias. However, she managed to get into the open window and I heard *thud* as she climbed in and promptly fell on the floor—phew! Of course, Heidi was laughing hysterically throughout this process as it was a bit of a surreal situation and we were both like drowned rats.

During our time in the Algarve, there were some unwritten rep rules that we all knew and lived by. One of which was that none of the reps would socialise with the holidaymakers as it was unprofessional and they were only there for a week or two. However, we all went to our local bars as there were lots of British people working in the resorts for the season so we got to know all of them and the locals too. As we were all quite spread out, we generally paired up and went out in twos and threes.

In 'my patch in the Old Town I had a few favourite places that I would visit endlessly and never get tired of. My favourite restaurant and bar of all time was sat on top of the tunnel that led down to the beach. It had the most amazing courtyard with a massive and very ancient looking lemon tree with gnarled branches growing in the middle of it and tables and chairs built around it. The walls were covered in typical blue and white Portuguese tiles with pictures of fishermen and there was an old well that sat at the side which had been made a feature of. This is where my love of swordfish came from as it was to die for. Freshly caught that day and cooked in lemon and garlic with loads of black pepper—I can almost smell it and taste it now. There was a bar attached to the restaurant that was indoors and covered in wood panelling like an English gentlemen's club and was a bit of a hideaway for me and the other reps as not many of our guests went there, but some of our friends worked behind the bar so we could really let our hair down—more than normal as our drinks were at a much-reduced rate.

If you should ever come across this pub, you should still find a pair of pink fluffy handcuffs hanging on a nail in the wall which we bought the owner for his birthday—but that's another story!

My second favourite place was a bar right in the middle of the square and, although there was nothing special about this bar, a few times a week there was live music; a guitarist and singer who I would sit and watch for hours and hours. He had the most amazing voice and when he played to you it was as if you were the only person in the room.

I was so excited when my dad and Ellen came to visit and I managed to get them a room in one of the hotels I worked in and gave them the best bedroom right at the top of the hotel. They were amazed at how many people I knew as we walked through the town and everyone waved or stopped for a chat. I think they had a good week and especially enjoyed the jeep safari I took them on and the evenings walking down the cobbles to listen to the live music following numerous delicious meals and copious amounts of rosé wine!

My sister and Arnold also came to visit, which was not as successful as they are a very bad influence on me (well that's what I tell myself!). It was near to the end of the season and I was extremely tired but wanted to have some fun with my sis. On one night out with them, I was enjoying myself so much that I may have had a bit too much to drink and gone to bed rather late, temporarily forgetting that the next day I was guiding an excursion that started with me getting on the coach at four thirty a.m. I'm sure you can guess the outcome. I overslept which is the one thing that you most definitely do not do when you are a rep and the biggest no-no going. Having woken up suddenly, I raced around feeling sick and still a bit drunk, trying to get dressed. Complete with hangover, I paid for a taxi to charge after the coach so I could get on board and take my guests out for the day which I did. It cost me a fortune—probably about two weeks' wages—but I hate letting people down and also didn't want to jeopardise my job. The worst bit, however, was yet to come as the day trip was on a boat, so green was the colour of my face all day—yuk.

I came back late that evening, longing for my bed and dry land and saw my sister and Arnold who filled me in on the rest of the evening once I had left them. All I can say is that I'm glad I left when I did, as they continued to drink more. Arnold realised that he had hot feet so decided to cool them down by climbing into the fountain in the centre of the town square and paddling around, whilst under the influence. Unfortunately for him, there were police patrolling the area who were not amused at the drunken English man with his trousers rolled up around his knees and threatened to arrest him. Luckily my sister managed to talk them out of it, and they were able to stagger back to their hotel to sleep it off—just as I was getting up.

Well, they have a good time wherever they go! Needless to say, that was the one and only time I have ever been late for anything in my entire life.

It was a bit of a surreal job as most people save hard for their two weeks in the sun each year, however, I was in a holiday bubble for ten months.

Some reps do get a bad reputation as they are just there to party and don't really care about the holidaymakers. They turn up late for their welcome meetings if they turn up at all, sometimes still drunk or at least very hungover. However, due to my age, I like to think that I was one of the more helpful reps and did really try to make sure they had a good time and took home good memories.

At the end of October, my time finally came to an end and Heidi and I went out for one last night with all our friends before I was due to fly home the next day. I stayed at her place as usual, however, I now think that Heidi had a bit of a problem with keys.

I'm not quite sure how she did it, but on the day I was due to fly home, she had managed to lock us into the apartment and, of course, she couldn't find the keys. The only way out was once again through the window but this time my suitcase had to come too! Heidi followed me out of the window as she was driving me around to say my goodbyes to everyone I had got to know over the year. I cried the whole way round, all the way to the airport and for the whole flight home. I landed back in the UK and went back to my Dad's house as I'd moved out of my rented place so that I didn't have to pay rent while I was away. The next morning was weird waking up in my old bedroom at home; no sun to get up to, no guests to go and greet and no plans for the evening so I was feeling a bit lost. It was as if the whole experience had been a dream and I had just woken up. It was very sad in one way being back, but lovely too as I could see my family and friends and it was definitely one of the best things I have ever done as I had so much fun and made some good friends. I really recommend it to everyone as it certainly makes you stand on your own two feet and quickly learn how to deal with situations. It was the best year, full of laughter.

I stayed good friends with Heidi and when we had both returned from Portugal from a year of sun, sea and sand, we decided that we needed a holiday. Hmmm where should we go? We needed to go somewhere completely different to where we had spent the last year so, after looking at a map, we came up with San Francisco!

It had begun—my life and love of travelling was just starting!

Chapter Six
San Francisco

Not yet having had enough of discovering exciting new places, my friend Heidi and I decided to go to America. The flight over was long and we were, of course, in the cheap seats and ended up at the back of the plane by the toilets enjoying the fragrances throughout the flight. Also, the seats didn't recline, so we were sat bolt upright for the duration, which was around eleven hours.

Of course, only having earned a few pounds a day in Portugal, the hotel we chose to stay at was ridiculously cheap, at twelve dollars each a night I guess we should have known it would not be the plushest of places; no pool, no spa but one thing we hadn't banked on was that we would be sharing our room with cockroaches. Each night, they would scuttle around the coving so we would make sure our heads were firmly in the pillow each night as sleeping or snoring with mouth open was not an option in case a cockroach dropped in.

The 'central location' advertised as a plus point on the hotel website obviously translated into the reality of a 'very noisy location' (a valuable lesson in reading between the lines) which was just by the turning circle of the trolley cars on Union Square. One special night, having been out for dinner and, of course, a few drinks, we were woken up by the sound of fire engines which we initially tried to ignore as, being on the main road, sirens were a frequent occurrence throughout the night. After a while of the constant noise getting louder, I decided that I had to get up and go and investigate. As I got close to the window, I almost had a heart attack as I saw a fireman looking back at me. Given we were on the seventh floor it was quite a shock, to which my reaction was jumping out of my skin and screaming.

"Oh my god there is a fireman at the window," I yelled at Heidi. The fireman peered into our room and shouted at us to get out of the building as it was on fire! If we had been timed, I am sure we would have made the *Guinness Book of World Records* as we have never got dressed so quickly and made it down seven flights of stairs in seconds to get out of the hotel. Having stood outside on the sidewalk for an hour, half dressed in pyjama bottoms and hoodies with party goers walking past in their evening frocks staring at us strangely, we were told that the fire was a false alarm. As usual, Heidi laughed all the way through the panic and drama which somehow made it OK. Thank goodness it was not a real fire as that was one adventure I didn't want on our holiday. Just another surreal and bizarre evening!

Heidi and I had planned to see as much as San Francisco as possible and we visited all the usual tourist attractions and especially enjoyed the wine tasting trip in the Napa Valley. We booked a trip on a minibus as obviously we didn't want to drive while surrounded by all that fantastic wine. As we stood in each vineyard and listened intensely to the technicalities of winemaking, we obviously necked as much alcohol as possible as it was included in the price. As we got louder and louder and Heidi laughed more and more, I think we lived up to the poor reputation of drunk Brits which did not go down too well with some of the older people in the group. But we had a great day and did still enjoy the most amazing scenery and fantastic wine, so it's definitely a must-do day trip if you ever get to go.

Yosemite National Park was on our list to visit and we hired a car, planning to drive there and back in a day which was a bit ambitious. As Heidi was the more competent of drivers on the 'wrong side' of the road, I very kindly nominated her to do all the driving which, luckily, she didn't mind at all. It was all going well and was quite straightforward on the smaller roads with not much traffic, however, when it came to getting on the freeway it was a different matter and suddenly, we realised that we had somehow got onto the freeway on the wrong side so were going the wrong way! It was then that I wasn't so sure about my decision to let Heidi do all the driving! As Heidi laughed her way through the episode, my heart was in my mouth seeing some oncoming cars in the distance, but she actually managed to get us off the freeway before they reached us; so we were unscathed and not arrested. The rest of the journey was fine and we enjoyed the most magical day in the most amazing and beautiful place with scenery that looked like a painting. There were massive cliffs that cricked your neck trying to see the top and that could have been man-made for rock climbers, huge grand trees that were surely hundreds of years old and the gorgeous smell of the forest; it was hard to believe that it was actually real and all of it made us feel very small and insignificant. Breathtaking. I wish we had the money and time to stay in one of the log cabins in the park which would have been superb, waking up in the middle of nature surrounded by stunning views but, you never know, maybe one day I will get back there. It's definitely another must-do trip if you are ever over that way, but a day trip is not long enough as we got back around one a.m.

We did all the usual shops and ate in cheap places with the locals and had such a fun time that, once again, the downers set in on the plane on the way back home. So, what were we going to do about it? Well, that was obvious. Another adventure of course! Hmmm… where should we go next as we could basically go anywhere in the world—well on a budget of course. How about skiing as neither of us had ever been? Too expensive maybe; but not in Romania!

This decision was made quickly and we both worked hard to try and save some money up, but it was very, very cheap indeed to go to Romania. Neither of us had any ski wear, which had to be purchased from the local market that, in hindsight, was probably not the best quality and certainly didn't keep me dry or warm but a small price to pay to be able to go skiing. I remember my first ski outfit well—an all-in-one jumpsuit—red with grey panels down the side made from sleeping bag type material that looked like all the air had been sucked out of it. Lovely.

Chapter Seven
Romania

WOW! What an amazing place Romania is and one of my favourites out of all the places that I have visited, as it was just so different. It was quite a while ago that we went and they had only just started receiving tourists so I imagine the hotels and resorts are probably a bit more geared up for it now.

Heidi and I were on a package holiday and as the flight had been delayed we arrived much later than anticipated so it was just starting to get dark. We got on the coach and started the journey to the hotel, looking around to see as much scenery as we could on the way. Excitement soon turned to fear as the coach driver narrowly missed several people with horse and carts that were driving in the middle of the road and then scared us to death by going way too fast up the winding mountains roads taking the tight bends on what felt like two wheels in the dark, snow and ice. My first skiing experience already had me in a panic! We were starving and cold, so we were really looking forward to our evening meal and very excited to get into the hotel. Unfortunately, the hotel staff had other ideas as we were late and they obviously wanted to go home. We sat down in the restaurant with all the staff standing around watching us in the hope we wouldn't stay, however, we were so hungry and as we didn't know where else to get food, plus it was included in the price so we were staying! Having ordered our meal, very quickly a couple of bowls of soup with a very strange and not very appetising greasy film on the top were plonked down on the table in front of us so we started to tuck in as though we hadn't eaten in days. About midway through our greasy soup, the lights went out in the restaurant and we were sat there in the dark trying to feel our way around our soup bowls! It seemed that all the staff had just left. Well, this started Heidi off with her infectious laugh which then started me off. We sat there for a while crying with laughter in disbelief and eventually, having finished our soup, felt our way around the walls to get out of the restaurant and went up to bed.

The next morning, we were ready to hit the slopes! Sporting our new gear, we collected our skis and excitedly but nervously made our way to our meeting point; at the time there were only about two slopes in the whole resort but that was absolutely fine for us novices.

The day was great and the instructor showed us the key moves including how to stop, which is obviously very important, so our confidence started to grow as we started to find our ski legs. So much so that the instructor decided to take us up to the top—the very top—of the mountain which, in hindsight and after a few more years of skiing, now I realise was just a big hill and nowhere near the mountain category. Either he thought we were better than we were, or he was bored of being on the nursery slopes and wanted a bit more excitement, adrenaline and probably a bit of a laugh at our expense! We quickly realised that this may be a bit above our skiing level and very sheepishly started to make our way down, trying to follow our instructor without falling over at every turn.

Two hours later, we were still very slowly making our way down, at which point our instructor was obviously really bored and just skied off. He shouted, "See you tomorrow", his voice fading as he sped off and disappeared over the brow of the hill. Another two hours later, and now in pitch darkness, we managed to get to the bottom. Having flown uncontrollably over the ice at the top of the mountain, scraping our skis on rocks and soil where the snow was thinning midway down, we ended up near the bottom trying to ski on grass so decided to take off our skis and walk, making a beeline for the lights of the pub where we sat down to rest our legs with a well earned glass of mulled wine; our knees throbbing, our muscles feeling like they were bursting out of our legs and our faces very red from being out in the elements for so long. It felt great to be in the warm even though our faces were now on fire and stinging from being so cold all day but, actually sitting down had never felt so good. Unfortunately, this was short-lived and it turns out not such a good idea as we found out when it came to getting up again. PAIN like I have never felt as we had totally ceased up!

We both hobbled back to our hotel, fighting to be the first in a hot bath and grabbing for the cans of Deep Heat, which we proceeded to spray thickly on our legs and which must have given everyone in our corridor a fume high but we would have done anything to relieve the pain. Was this supposed to be fun? I couldn't quite see it at this point and started to have a bit of a sense of humour failure, however, as usual Heidi started laughing which instantly made everything all right.

The following morning and, due to the previous day's mammoth expedition, neither of us could move our legs or get out of bed but we had another lesson booked so weren't going to miss it.

It took a bit longer to get all our gear on, however, finally off we went, determined to enjoy ourselves: which we did. Ice, grass, seeing someone fall off a chair lift; it was all part of the holiday and another funny memory (obviously not for the person that fell of the lift but I think they were OK).

As usual, we wanted to see the country as well as learn to ski, so went on a number of excursions while we were in Romania. It was such a different place to anywhere I had ever been.

I have always had a fascination for those old black and while Dracula films with Christopher Lee and Peter Cushing and am an avid fan of the Hammer Horror movies. I always felt that I should have lived in one of those big old-fashioned castles with roaring open fires, secret passages and torches hung on the giant doors outside to light the dark and scary cobbled streets.

So Romania, home of Vlad Dracul, Vlad the Impaler AKA Count Dracula and where all the stories came from, made the perfect place for me to visit. I just had to go on a day trip to the Castle of Dracula while I was there—how scary! Unfortunately, it turned out that the castle we were taken to, which looked like it had been built from an Ikea flat pack, wasn't the actual castle of Dracula. This one was especially for the tourists and you could see the modern carpentry on the new light-coloured wooden beams. I was not impressed, however, I did learn a lot on the trip including why Vlad was called the Impaler as he used to put rows of wooden stakes outside his castle to defend it, so anyone running up to the castle would be impaled on them. Fascinating, yes? I thought so. The real Count Dracula's castle is apparently inaccessible by road and can only be reached by a helicopter transfer which we couldn't afford, however, this is the one I really want to see—the photos look amazing—a dark, grey, Gothic building up on the top of a hill being circled by large bats, where you can imagine the large rooms with their cold stone floors lit by huge candles and imposing fireplaces—very eerie.

However, it was not to be so I guess I will have to make do with the old films, which are still my favourites today.

While our muscles were still recovering, we decided to take another day trip and visit Ceauşescu's palace in Bucharest, which stands proud at the top of many steps and is lavished inside and out with gold. It is a place of pure extravagance and you lose yourself in the beauty and splendour while inside.

Bucharest seems to be a place of two halves. The grandeur of the palace with modern roads and buildings at the front, but if you walk down the side streets of the palace and around the back, out of the sight of the main entrance, you find the other extreme, which was a bit shocking.

There were cobbled streets, old-fashioned street lanterns and old-style shop fronts that looked like a scene from a Charles Dickens film. At that time, there was thick snow on the floor, glistening in the sun with the background of blue sky. The amazing buildings looked beautiful and we were really enjoying our visit, that was until we came across the children who had no shoes on, many of whom were on crutches with various limbs missing. It was like the Dark Ages and a huge contrast to the wealth of the palace and the new city out front. The children were sent over to us by their parents to beg for money or food as we stood out a mile as obvious Westerners which, in their eyes, meant that we had lots of money although we didn't, however, in comparison we were kings. It was so sad to see and these scenes were just yards from where the Grand Palace stood but kept out of sight of most tourists.

I know every city has its divides and I'm sure and really hope that now it is a different story. I would so love to go back to visit again as it is a special and intriguing place, but would really love to get to the true Count Dracula's castle...

Once again, it was time to come home, move on in my life and settle down a bit. Heidi didn't live very close to me and she got on with her own life, getting married, having twins and generally doing grown-up and responsible things which, unfortunately, means we haven't seen each other for years.

Chapter Eight
Back to base

Being back home and back to normality once again was quite depressing, however, following my exciting and surreal experience as a holiday rep and my recent holidays, I decided I enjoyed the whole hospitality and travel lifestyle so applied for a job in an event agency. To my amazement, I got the job where my events career really started.

I was very excited to start my new job even though it was not initially working on the events but helping the sales team, however, it was a foot in the door and the longer I was there, the more I got involved in the events and in particular the corporate hospitality side—the best side in my opinion—which fuelled my interest more. Well, who calls taking groups of clients out to Chelsea Flower Show and on the most gorgeous boats for a sailing day work? Not me!

It was at this company, gosh, a very long time ago now which is a very scary thought, where I met Fiona and Simone who I am still friends with now.

Fiona is lovely, she is one of the most kind and thoughtful people you will ever meet. A funny old stick who is enthusiastic about everything and never has a bad word to say about anyone. A tall girl with hair not too dissimilar to mine in texture so we always both have a moan when it's raining as our hair grows upwards and outwards in a big frizz ball in virtual synchronisation. As an outdoorsy type, she generally dresses in practical clothing, usually wearing a big brimmed bushman's hat, a long, waxed coat and long brown waterproof boots making her look like the local woodsman, but in a lovely and style icon way.

She lives with her husband, Bruce, in a gorgeous barn-style house with a very high vaulted ceiling and wooden floors, surrounded by farmland where she keeps a horse, dogs, bees and she even had a very large pig who was very cute. Sadly, none are with us any longer, however, she has children to look after instead now!

Occasionally she works as a garden designer but also offers her time for voluntary work including having elderly people round for lunches, coffee afternoons and for Christmas dinners. Fiona is very knowledgeable about virtually everything and has the most amazing memory. She often takes tour groups around the local gardens and knows every plant's Latin name as well as its common name—I have no idea how she remembers them all! She has a very intelligent, kind, lovely husband in Bruce, and I often get lost when in conversations with them both as they use words that I have never heard of, so I politely nod and smile as if I know what they are talking about and then rush home to the dictionary!

Whenever I am not working, we meet up to walk her dogs in the woods that surround us where we live and then always have a coffee. If only I could do that every week, I would be in my element and I would never get bored of how different the trees, plants and woods look during each season. Fiona, and especially Bruce, are amazing skiers; Bruce having preiouvsly worked as a ski guide so he is very advanced.

Simone is also lovely—a very pretty girl—blonde and thin who is into all the latest music and movies and now works in that industry, which is perfect for her.

Just like me, Simone was single for a while after she broke up with a boyfriend many years ago. It is hard to meet people as it really is highly unlikely to meet anyone that is a good match in a bar or nightclub and, as the company where we worked was mainly women, that too was an unlikely place to meet someone.

However, we did all go out clubbing quite a lot, in fact most weekends as we both loved a dance, and to the same place in Windsor as we knew the regular crowd there so it was guaranteed that we would always get in and could even sometimes jump the queue! The venue is still there but is now a different type of club that I would not frequent. It stands under the railway arches that are like an aqueduct so it's a weird shape but it was such a cool space. On entry, you would queue down the stairs but couldn't see into the club, so the anticipation would grow as we waited to get in and listened to the pounding music and the hubbub of the crowds already inside. We used to stand in the same place each time we visited—the highest point at the top bar so we could survey the room. We used to dance to the same eighties' club classics each week, requesting the same records over and over again, such as Todd Terry and Jocelyn Brown, 'Somebody Else's Guy' (bring back memories?), that we never got bored of. Worst of all, we used to drink the same drink each week that I certainly couldn't face now—strawberry vodka shots—which at the time we used to love, with intermittent Long Island iced teas that used to blow our heads off! When I think of the quantities and mixtures of drinks I used to consume, I still feel the need for a detox!

One evening we had drunk rather a lot of alcohol and my high heels were killing me so the thought of walking all the way home was not appealing. On the way out of the club, a police car was sitting there, just in case of any trouble I guess, so I thought I would cheekily try my luck as we walked past and stuck my head in the window, said, 'hello', and then told my pathetic story about my poor feet hurting and how far we would have to walk so asked if we could get a lift home. To my surprise and the amazement of my friends, they said yes! We all piled in to the police car and got a free ride home in style! I'm guessing they said yes as we were rather intoxicated and it was probably the safest option, but who cares as it saved my feet and, if you don't ask, you don't get! Thank you very much to the Windsor police!

I feel very lucky to have friends that I have kept in touch with for years, who I can meet up with even if we have not seen or spoken with each other for months and it is as if no time has passed. Both Fiona and Simone turned out to be very, very good life long friends that I am very lucky to have.

Back at work I got more and more involved in the actual events rather than the sales side and really enjoyed working there, however, after a good stint, once again I felt it was time to move on.

My twenties were spent moving around jobs to find my 'career path', if you can call it that, and moving house which I did numerous times but always in Windsor and always renting a room so meeting new housemates and making loads of new friends. I made sure that each house I lived in was always within walking distance of the town and its bustling nightlife. As you can probably tell, I was a bit of a party animal in my younger days—well, I guess I was just enjoying myself—and I can certainly say that I had the best time ever living in Windsor.

In one of the houses I lived in, I met two more very good friends, Emilia and Daisy, who also rented a room in the same house. It was quite a large house with an enormous garden and situated down a private road which meant we actually had parking: a rarity in the centre of Windsor. The house was a bit tatty as its four bedrooms had been rented out for so long it was looking a bit worse for wear, however, the location made up for it. It was a typical shared house where we all had a cupboard each in the kitchen and our own shelf in the fridge and unfortunately only one bathroom (that had a very old-fashioned yellow coloured suite which I can say I have never seen before nor wish to again) which was interesting when we were all trying to get ready for work in the mornings. However, we had such fun living together for a good few years and great times that I will never forget as we were constantly laughing and didn't seem to have a care in the world. It's funny how, even though I earnt very little money, had to pay rent and bills, I still seemed to live like a king and have quite a bit of disposable income to go out all the time.

Daisy is one of those people who is great to be around. She is full of energy and optimism, which seems to be a trait that all my friends share and the type of person I like to be around. She is extremely funny and I do miss not seeing her that often.

It was actually Daisy's suggestion that I write a book as I always had a story to tell about something that had happened to me, so thank you to her for the idea!

Daisy is taller than me (which is not difficult!) with shoulder length brown hair and doesn't wear much make-up as she doesn't need it. She has such a funny and very dry sense of humour and once tried to organise a fancy-dress party at our rented house—the rule of attendance being that everyone had to dress up like our landlord i.e., wearing a bald wig and glasses. He used to just appear quite frequently at the end of the garden through an archway leading to his house next door, so it would have been so hysterically funny if he had turned up in the garden to find twenty other people looking just like him! Needless to say, no one bought into the idea but it did make me laugh.

Emilia also had a very dry sense of humour which sometimes took me by surprise as her comments were so sharp and witty, she would catch me off-guard. Annoyingly, Emilia had a mass of lovely bright red curly hair that, unlike mine, never seemed to go frizzy.

Emilia and Daisy are both very clever people but also very down to earth and just 'get on with it' rather than moaning about things, which I have to admit I am not great at. I do sometimes whinge although I make a conscious effort not to and am getting better!

One of the funniest days out with Emilia was one of our many trips to London to watch the Oxford and Cambridge boat race. It was an annual outing for me, along with whoever I could talk into coming too, as it was always an enjoyable day watching the race and, of course, soaking up the atmosphere and enjoying a few glasses of wine out in the sunshine along the way, which always helped the day along nicely. No surprise there then.

Emilia had moved out of our rented place by this time and in with her boyfriend although they still lived in Windsor so we set off for London for a good day out, leaving her boyfriend at home as he was planning to have a game of golf with his mates and then do the monthly food shop. What a great boyfriend!

We arrived at Hammersmith riverside which was absolutely heaving with people—ten-deep in places to reach the river wall so we couldn't actually see that much. We watched what we could and the roar of the crowd told us when the boats were coming. Unfortunately, we assumed the first cheer was the race when, in actual fact, it was the junior crew in the pre-race and we actually missed the main race as we were queuing for a drink. However, Oxford did not win which I was disappointed at, even though there is no real reason I was supporting them. As usual, the British weather kicked in and from lovely sunshine, it started to rain so we headed back into the bar for shelter, along with a few hundred other people.

With the noise of the crowds, the music and entertainment plus probably the effects of a few drinks, we didn't hear Emilia's phone ringing, and ringing, and ringing. Later that afternoon she checked her messages and realised she had a number of calls from her boyfriend, progressively getting more and more desperate and asking when she would be back as she had taken his house key so he couldn't get in.

We aimed to leave London at a certain time to catch the train back so we didn't get home too late to let Emilia's boyfriend in, however, the drinks were flowing rather too well and we got a bit sidetracked by having way too much fun.

As we were having such a good time, we didn't realise that it had got dark and, given this was summer, it was obviously quite late. In fact, last orders were called at which point we ran out of the pub back to the train station and only just managed to get the last train back.

We made it back, goodness knows how, and got a taxi from the train station. Emilia was dropped off first at her flat and must have gone straight upstairs, into the flat and passed out on the bed—completely forgetting about her boyfriend.

Very early the next morning, she was awoken to loud banging on the door which startled her from her hungover slumber. She flew down the stairs, still wearing the clothes from the day before with big black panda eyes from the previous day's make-up to see what on earth the noise was.

She opened the door to and, to her horror, saw her boyfriend standing there looking rather worse for wear, clutching four supermarket bags that were dripping on the floor with once frozen food that had defrosted. He had slept in the car all night as he didn't see her arrive back, and his knocking on the door in the early hours fell on deaf and drunken ears.

He was not amused and I'm sure still holds me responsible for being a bad influence on his girlfriend which was obviously not true at all. I, however, found this extremely funny and had to tell everyone I knew the whole story over and over again. I think Emilia's boyfriend can laugh about it now, but only just.

Needless to say, we haven't been to the boat race together since but I highly recommend it as it is great fun!

Daisy also normally had a funny story to tell. Now with a husband and three children, she works teaching languages as she is very clever and still continues to make us laugh in her own unique way!

One of her stories was during an outing to take her daughter swimming at the local pool. You would wonder what could possibly go wrong, but she hadn't been to this particular pool before which was also a conference venue complete with bar, meeting rooms and gym.

Having packed all their swimming gear, driven to the pool and then got herself and her daughter changed into their swimming togs—all which takes time with a toddler as I'm sure a lot of you know—Daisy locked their belongings in the locker and they were all set for a swim. As she looked around for the entrance to the pool, she realised that there were four doors within the changing room, none of which had any signs attached so she was not sure which way to go to get to the pool. She chose one, thinking she would have a peek and if it did not lead to the pool then she would try another. Unfortunately, the door she chose was a heavy fire door and, as her daughter was excited to get in the water, she rushed through. Daisy followed and, within seconds of the heavy fire door banging shut behind her, realised that this was totally the wrong door as she was standing in the middle of the public bar in her swimming costume. Even more unfortunate was that the bar was busy due to a function at the venue and it was packed with people in business suits. With everyone staring at her, she hurridly grabbed her daughter to get back into the changing room and pulled on the door they had come through, to her horror realising that as a fire door it only opened one way so she could not get back in. To make things even worse (if that were possible), Daisy asked the bar staff which way she needed to go to get back to the pool and it turned out that the only way to get back round to the correct entrance was to go outside and around the building. Barefoot, on the gravel and in her swimming costume, she made her way around to the entrance, closely followed by security cameras that were tracking her every move. I bet the security guards were having such a laugh. How very cringy. Only Daisy.

Both Emilia and Daisy now have children and partners and, although we only manage to meet up once or twice a year, I know we will keep in touch for the rest of our lives.

I made some really good forever friends during this time, however, I was still not content with just squeezing in a few hours of frantic sightseeing in between events while travelling with work and I wanted to go everywhere in the world and explore properly. I had already had some great holidays and I'm sure that everyone has great memories and tales to tell from holidays they took in their twenties as they do seem to be the best holidays that we all remember very fondly; sometimes through rose tinted glasses, but who cares.

I certainly knew how to have fun and, looking back, I have been lucky to go on so many work trips and holidays. When you are young you are not so fussy about where you stay as long as it is the cheapest option possible, even so, everything seemed cheaper and much more accessible back in the good old eighties, didn't it?

One of the perks working in event agencies, apart from the travelling, is that I was able to get travel and holiday discounts which I took full advantage of and visited places like Barbados and France on reduced rates. However, I was quite adventurous and, along with the usual beach holidays which were fantastic, I liked to try different places that were not in your standard holiday brochure. There are a few that follow which stuck in my mind for various reasons but all were good fun and I definitely recommend them all!

Chapter Nine
Norway

This is probably not everyone's first choice of location when booking a holiday, however, I decided it would be fun to go for a long weekend with Emilia. I'm not sure why I thought of Norway, maybe I saw a TV programme on it or something, but it turned out to be a great choice! Of course it would have been lovely to go in the summer so we could enjoy all the amazing scenery and the great outdoors but, as usual, we decided to be different and, as money was tight, we decided to go in November when it was really cheap—not surprisingly as it is one of the coldest months in the northern hemisphere. Cold was an understatement: it was freezing. Emilia and I got off the plane wrapped up in our warm coats, gloves and hats and boarded our transfer. As we were getting close to where we were staying—a city on the west coast called Bergen, we looked out of the coach window at the glistening icy rivers and snow-capped mountains as we drove past, wiping the windows that were steaming up with our warm breath. It was such a beautiful place and we wanted to see as much as we could during our short stay, so we wasted no time in booking an excursion as soon as we arrived. Once again, I'm not quite sure why, but instead of a nice warm sightseeing coach trip somewhere, stopping off for cups of coffee and seeing the highlights in comfort, we decided that it would be a great idea to book white-water rafting…

Oh, my goodness what were we thinking— obviously we weren't thinking at all! I don't think we had realised that we were actually going to have to get in the water, unless we were unlucky enough to fall in, and we were going to be in a boat so surely, we wouldn't get wet at all? We arrived at the rafting centre and registered our names and stood ready for the briefing. Everything started off well. The guys running the rafting were smiling and friendly, however, not long into the briefing, and to our utter shock and horror, we were given wet woolly jumpers that were so icy and cold they were stiff as boards and didn't smell too fresh. We were told that we had to wear them under a cold, wet, icy wetsuit—nooooo! The jumper was supposedly to keep us warm but I think the instructors were actually just having a laugh at our expense as I noticed they were not wearing them. This was already not my idea of a fun afternoon out but, at the time, I just got on with it and I was sure it would be fun when we got out on the water and another new activity that I could cross off my list.

Straight after the jumper shock we were told to pick up a pair of gloves as the water was so cold that we could get frostbite… this was not helping the fun aspect of my afternoon. They say things happen in threes and, unfortunately, the third shocker was we were then given instructions to jump in the river and swim upstream against the flow of water to prove that we could swim properly in case we fell out of the raft. Once again, I'm sure this was the instructors amusing themselves but we did as we were told and jumped in. The shock alone of jumping into such cold water made me hyperventilate and gave me such a head spin I thought I was going to pass out and drown. During all of this, I was thinking and wondering why we had actually paid good money to do this but that actually spurred me on to try and enjoy myself and learn something new.

Having completed this task, we scrambled out of the river and dried off as much as possible to get warm. It was then all a bit of a rush to jump in the boats and set off downstream into the rapids so as not to not waste any of our 'fun' time, so we grabbed our gloves and took them into the boat with us. Off we went, paddling frantically and finally starting to have fun and a few laughs. However, our hands were getting wet with the icy water as we hadn't had time to put our gloves on so they were starting to turn a kind of blue-orange colour that looked like the 'corned beef' pattern that my legs used to look like while walking to school in the snow in a short skirt and ankle socks. Emilia yelled at me to put my gloves on, which I did, while still trying to paddle against the strong water. Unfortunately, in my haste to get in the boat, I realised that I had picked up two left-hand gloves and started to have a slight panic. I turned to Emilia and showed her my hands, one with a glove on and the other one completely blue, while also holding up the other glove to show her what I had done. Expecting some sympathy and, of course, the offer from her to share her right-hand glove with me, Emilia instead burst into hysterical laughter that lasted for most of the journey and never once offered to lend me her glove. The whole incident was so amusing to Emilia, especially when she then compared me to Michal Jackson with his one white glove and insisted on calling me 'Michael' for the rest of the weekend, whilst doing an impression.

Still to this day, she often does her 'Michael' impression when she sees me and. at one of her birthday parties that was fancy dress, I indulged her and went along as Michael with my one glove which went down a treat!

After thinking that I was either going to drown or get frostbite in my fingers, our efforts were rewarded as they had filmed us for the company's promotional video which I am sure it is still out there somewhere, although I must have looked ridiculous! And it was actually good fun.

For the last full day of our weekend away, we decided to take things a bit easier and go on a boat trip to see the beautiful fjords. As we waited to board the boat, we had our photo taken by a life-size statue of a troll on the jetty. Norway has ancient folklores that say trolls once lived in the forests, only coming out at night to roam around as the daylight would hurt them. They were odd looking things; with crazy hair and long noses they could sometimes be dangerous but some could also be very friendly as the stories go. There are lots of tales about trolls and some believe that they still exist today.

We got on board the large ferry-style boat and, as we sailed off, we huddled inside to keep warm as it was freezing. Even though it was bright sunshine with the most amazing clear blue skies, we would only go out on deck when we were approaching a sightseeing landmark. With the cold air making it difficult to get our breath, the boat sailed around the corner where the most magnificent sight greeted us. There was a beautiful corridor of icy water, crystal blue with a tinge of green, with walls of snow-capped mountains on each side towering above us that looked like they were closing in on us as we sailed through. I felt like Kirk Douglas in the film *The Vikings*.

To see the fjords really finished our Norwegian adventure on a high. The people were lovely, the scenery amazing and beautiful and I would definitely recommend visiting although take your own alcohol if you want a drink in your room as it is very expensive… but what a great trip!

Chapter Ten
Bangkok and Bali

Back at home I was just sitting in the lounge one day in our house in Windsor watching TV and Daisy walked in and announced that she was moving out as she was going travelling for a year with an old friend from university. What! I was really shocked as I hadn't heard anything about this and both Emilia and myself were very sad that she was leaving as life in the house would not be the same without her. However, our disappointment was short-lived and we very quickly got over this shock news as her next sentence immediately cheered us up when she asked if Emilia and I would like to meet them somewhere along their route for a holiday! We didn't need to be asked twice and immediately started planning!

We were so excited and sat down to look through their itinerary as they had already planned where they were going to visit, which was the Far East. We went through their route and places they had wanted to stop and visit to decide where we should go and meet them. Well, it wasn't a difficult decision. The place we chose to meet up with them was Bali. I had never been to the Far East and it sounded like a right adventure. Our planning started for what was, initially, a week away, however, this then got extended into a two-week holiday as we decided to spend a few days in Bangkok as a stopover beforehand. After all, it was a long way to go so we should make the most of it!

As per usual money was tight so we scoured the travel agent brochures for the cheapest flights and accommodation possible and got everything booked. The time came for Daisy to leave and, as we sadly said goodbye to Daisy with her rucksack on her back ready for her adventure, we were willing the time to pass quickly as we were so excited about our trip and our own adventure.

Over the next few weeks, we had a few postcards from Daisy but not really much contact, but finally the time arrived for Emilia and I to go and meet with her. The flight was long, stuck in the middle seat in the very back row as per usual it seemed, so no possibility to recline, but we were finally on our way with a mixture of excitement and nerves as we didn't really know what to expect. We landed in Bangkok and got off the plane wondering what would greet us. To our amazement and total surprise (although I don't know why), we found Bangkok airport to be the cleanest and shiniest airport I've ever seen; gleaming white floors, light and airy and air conditioned. How lovely.

Feeling a bit more reassured, we walked outside— bam! The humidity hit us in the face like a brick wall. The air felt so thick and I couldn't breathe properly which, in a strange sort of way, all added to the excitement as the nerves returned, suddenly realising we were in a completely different country, different culture and different climate to where we had come from.

We were only in Bangkok for a long weekend, so we decided, as usual, to pack it full and do as much as possible.

Emilia convinced me to take the obligatory ride in a tuk-tuk, as you do when you are in Bangkok. Well, I know I am a bit of a wimp when it comes to roller coasters and I hate speed full stop, but this really was something else and I was petrified, as the driver was a maniac! We were weaving in and out of the traffic, squeezing between cars, lorries and cyclists. The buses were the worst though, apart from the sheer size of them and us being lower down than the height of the bus wheels, we were sat at exhaust pipe level so each time a bus drove off, we were plunged into large plumes of grey exhaust smoke and spent the next five minutes coughing while hanging on as we couldn't see anything in front of us, let alone the driver. We were still managing to smile—well more of a grimace on my part—but the next fright was the final straw as, when we whizzed round a corner, one of the three wheels on the tuk-tuk actually left the ground leaving us balancing on one back wheel, wobbling as we took the bend. I rapidly clambered onto Emilia's lap to get all our weight back on the other side as I was sure we were going to topple over. I was not happy and did have a bit of a sense of humour failure which Emilia found highly amusing—of course—and has delighted in telling everyone ever since. I can laugh about it now, many years later, but that was another experience that I would not repeat. Ever.

Having survived the day, the other item on our itinerary was a day trip to the famous floating market which I have seen on many travel programmes and was a must-do on the holiday. Oh, my goodness it was the funniest thing ever and I definitely got my own back on Emilia with this one. I think most people know of the floating markets from brochures or the TV—made up of lovely wooden boats carrying fruit, vergetables or other wares for sale, gently being paddled along the serene waterways by small old men in large floppy hats to keep out the sun.

We thought it would be nice to take a trip in one of these boats that were for the tourists, stopping at a few of the riverside huts en route to purchase some souvenirs while enjoying the sights and smells of the flowers and food that lined the water.

But, no, how wrong we were—again.

We stepped into a long and fairly narrow boat only seating one person on each side and around ten people in total, paid the man for the journey and sat down. I couldn't see the paddles at this point but I wasn't really paying too much attention, however, the next thing I knew, the driver had shuffled to the back of the boat and was yanking a cord as though he was starting an engine. How weird, I thought. To our surprise, we soon found out that we had been correct in our observations and a bit slow to realise that the cord was in actual fact attached to a motor that had not one but two exhaust pipes attached to this flimsy and lightweight wooden boat! Oh, my goodness—we shot off like a cannonball—the front of the boat was high out of the water and the back almost submerged, the smoke bellowing from the exhaust and leaving a great wake in our trail with us hanging on for dear life. It was just like a James Bond film!

Ha ha; it was payback time for Emilia's tuk-tuk ride, as we sped along the water she was laughing so much, mouth wide open, she ingested a mouthful of river water as it sprayed up from the boat's edge. I am not sure what is in the Bangkok River but I'm guessing it is definitely not for drinking. Luckily, she was OK but, oh, how I laughed—and laughed—and laughed and, of course, I had to tell everyone!

What an amazing place Bangkok is; even walking around the town was an experience in itself. Hot and humid with so many people; the smell of cooking drifting from the food stalls lining the pavements and incense sticks burning made the atmosphere completely different to anything I had experienced before. As we looked for somewhere to eat, I saw something out of the corner of my eye which made me do a double take. I thought I was seeing things as there was an elephant on the pavement! Not only that, it was standing at a cash point machine and using his trunk to press the buttons! Yes really! Maybe I had drunk something that was making me see things: possibly the river water. To my relief, we then saw that there was a trainer with him but still very odd indeed and something you wouldn't see in most other major cities!

Emilia and I did the whole tourist thing and visited temples, saw the famous gold lying down Buddha and went to a night market which was certainly an eye-opener given some of the shops, what they were selling and the shows on offer. All I will say is 'ping pong balls' which may give you an idea if you have heard anything about the interesting Bangkok nightlife! We certainly made the most of our time there even though the trip itself was short.

It was soon time to fly to Bali to meet Daisy and her friend which was very exciting, so we packed up and got to the airport and it was only a four-hour flight so not too bad. We landed quite late and, by the time we had got to our hotel, to our distress our room had been given away to someone else and there were no other rooms spare—aarrghh! Just what you don't want when you arrive in a foreign country in the middle of the night. Fortunately, the hotel took responsibility and shipped us off to another hotel for one night, much to our annoyance, as we were due to meet Daisy. I made sure that the hotel knew our friend was coming to meet us and asked them to let Daisy know where we had gone, although I wasn't sure that our message would actually be delivered.

At the new hotel, which wasn't far from the one we had actually booked, Emilia and I decided that there wasn't much we could do about our situation that night so went down to the bar for a drink, bearing in mind that only the man on reception knew that we had been moved to a new hotel so we thought it unlikely we would see our friend. This new location was amazing. What an incredible setting, sitting outside in the lush and tropical gardens of a hotel bar in the middle of nowhere, in a country halfway around the world enjoying a cold beer in the humidity of the night and listening to the unfamiliar wildlife which was kind of nice but also a bit scary at the same time as I am not a bug lover. The telephone at the bar started to ring but, of course, we didn't pay much attention until the barman walked out from behind his bar asking for, "Miss Kate". The call was for me! How surreal—a phonecall for me on the other side of the world—I felt like an MI5 agent being contacted with a secret message, or a celebrity, as everyone was staring wondering who I was as the barman asked if I would accept the call!

Of course, it was Daisy as she had called our original hotel and the man on reception had very kindly put her through to where we were staying for the night. We re-arranged when and where to meet and then went off to bed. How funny.

The next day, all four of us met up. It was great to see them and it was if we hadn't seen each other for years as we were all so excited. I did feel a bit sorry for Daisy's travelling companion; a man that we didn't really know but he was so easy to get on with and a great sport in joining in. We discussed what we would like to do and decided to hire a man with a van to drive us around the island so we could do some sightseeing without the pressure of one of us having to drive and navigate the roads and the local drivers. It was ridiculously cheap, so we planned our route and made the arrangements. The man with the van who we had not yet met, turned out to be the cousin of our hotel receptionist. Probably not a very sensible idea in hindsight, but there were four of us so we thought it would be OK.

One of the places on our list to visit was an area called Tanah Lot in the north of the island. WOW! And double WOW! This is the most amazing and mystical place I think I have ever seen. I will never forget the image of stunning temples sitting in front of a calm sea, with a background of eery mist lingering just above the water and a dark and moody sky—maybe this is where the saying comes from, the calm before the storm as I was sure we were in for a torrential downpour at any minute. Combined with the strong smell of incense sticks burning all around, it was a truly wonderful and, I would even go so far as to say, a magical moment.

We spent quite a long time here, as it was just so stunning, we didn't want to leave. During our visit we saw the locals bringing out small flower baskets with incense sticks, placing them at either side of the pathway lining a route to the water. We thought there may be a wedding taking place, but it turned out to be a funeral. What a lovely tranquil send off.

Sadly, it was time to leave Tanah Lot so we all jumped back into the van when the driver asked whether we minded if we took a detour to his mother's house as he needed pick something up. Of course, it was fine and, when we got to the house, we all waited in the back of the van trying to take a peek into all of the nearby properties as we had gone off the beaten track so wanted to see how everyone really lived. We were back on the road within a short time and, as we drove along enjoying the scenery, I thought I heard a strange noise. It sounded like clucking. Emilia had obviously heard it too as we turned and looked at each other. We automatically blamed Daisy as we thought she was making chicken noises just for some fun as this was something she would do. This went on for about ten minutes and, having constantly bombarded Daisy with blame, to our horror the driver said that his collection from his mother's house was some live chickens that were now in the boot! I am an animal lover and Daisy is a vegetarian so you can imagine our reactions to this. Many questions fired out of our mouths aimed at the driver. What are you doing with them? Are they OK in the back? Are you going to keep them as pets? (Highly unlikely and wishful thinking on our part.) Are you going to sell them? Worst case scenario: are you going to kill them and eat them?

We were so relieved at our driver's answer when he said he wouldn't eat them. However, this was to be a short-lived feeling as he then went on to say, "I am going to fight them!" How awful, but there was obviously nothing we could do, and this was a long time ago so I am sure it doesn't happen now.

It was a very quiet journey back to the hotel as we were all a bit shocked and upset.

The rest of our stay was great, back in our originally booked hotel with a pool and swim up bar! We went out and about, wandering around, soaking up the atmomsphere. I had always wanted to get a dress made as I had heard amazing things about the tailors in this part of the world so found somewhere that took my measurements and exact deails of the dress I wanted.

Unfortunately, Emilia got a very bad bug and was bathroom bound for a few days, so I spent time by the pool enjoying the sun.

It was finally time to leave and return home. It was very sad saying goodbye to Daisy and her friend, but we knew we would meet up when she got back.

I went to collect my new dress which, to my disappointment, wasn't ready. The shop promised to send it to me, although I wasn't convinced, I would ever see it.

Back home and the post holiday blues set in for a while, but I then received a package in the post which was my dress! Oh, how exciting as it had brought the whole holiday back to life. I ripped open the package and saw a lovely dress in the nice linen material I had picked out and immediately wanted to put it on. Unfortunately, I could hardly get one leg in it, let alone the whole of my body as it was way too small. Very, very disappointing in a funny sort of way.

I will never forget this holiday with my two great friends.

Chapter Eleven
Settling down and late found love

Back home and back to normal once again. I was still renting a room in a shared house and had got to the stage where I decided it was time to try and get on the property ladder, mainly so I could have all the shelves in the fridge to myself and didn't have to share a bathroom. I loved Windsor but could never have afforded to live anywhere near, let alone in the town centre. Even the one-bedroom flats were way out of my price range, so the options were to either move to somewhere less desirable and own my own place or stay renting and effectively waste money paying someone else's mortgage for them.

The decision was to bite the bullet and buy a house in a 'less than desirable area', to say the very least. I looked at all areas and the cheapest, which many people describe as, "the outskirts of Windsor", more commonly known as Slough, was the chosen destination. Now don't get me wrong, we have all seen and cringed at the concrete jungle pictures of Slough roundabout and bus station at the beginning of *The Office* but some parts are lovely. However, unfortunately for me to buy a house, the location I could afford was not lovely and, in fact, probably the worst place possible. The house, a two-bedroom ex-council house, was a great house actually and really well built, however, it was adorned by a charming pebble-dashed front and there was lots of dog mess on the pavement when I went for the viewing, as pointed out by the estate agent which I thought was not the best sales tactic. The house was situated in the middle of a notorious housing estate that regularly appeared on police documentaries on TV with residents of that particular road fighting and wielding machetes. On entering the house, it was clear that there was no central heating and the five bolts on the front door should have set my alarm bells ringing. However, this was the reality of what I could afford so I said, 'yes', and gave myself two years to do it up and move out, hopefully making some money in the meantime to enable me to move back to my beloved Windsor. I think my dad was quite surprised at my decision when he saw it but kept his opinion to himself, thankfully.

I only made cosmetic changes; the walls were all a dark burnt orange so I painted them lemon yellow which I'm sure was an 'in' colour at that time, plus put some new carpet down. I tidied up the front and back gardens which took a very long time as it was a very large garden—one hundred feet, in fact—but completely overgrown and covered in rubbish that had been left or thrown over by the neighbours.

The neighbours… always check out the neighbours before you buy a house as this can, and should be, a

127

major factor in your decision to buy. This was a valuable lesson I learnt and will never forget and never repeat. My new neighbours turned out to be a family comprising of three grown-up brothers all in their early twenties, their mother and numerous animals: a large dog, parrots, rabbits and goodness knows what else, all squashed into a two-bedroom house. I have to say there were some strange goings on, with people knocking on their door at all hours throughout the night which led me to believe they were up to no good but not the type of people you would question, especially following our first few conversations, one consisting of the line, "We quite like you so we will make sure none of our friends break into your house". I smiled and laughed nervously as I actually thanked them. What was I thinking? My deadline to do the house up and move back to Windsor was now my main and urgent focus.

Living there was not the most uplifting of experiences, putting up with constant noise from next door, having to make sure that I bolted all five locks on the door every night and it was actually quite depressing driving home from work each day as it really wasn't a nice place to be. However, two years and two weeks later (two weeks past my deadline) I sold the house! I was very lucky as I made some profit and was finally able to start climbing the property ladder and move back to Windsor. Well, maybe it wasn't central Windsor, but I was getting closer and the location was classed as West Windsor which was a lifetime away from the road I lived on in Slough. I was able to afford another ex-council place which was very sturdy and well-built with quite large rooms, high ceilings and big windows that let loads of light in. This time it was a two bedroomed maisonette with a very small front garden and it didn't need much doing to it but, again, I put down new carpets and painted the walls—magnolia this time which was much better than yellow and again the colour of the moment. Ahhh, home at last! Well, nearly.

The timing was key as deposits required were low, making it much easier for more people to get on the property ladder and make money from buying and selling which I know is much harder now.

So, now in my thirties, all grown-up and living near Windsor in my own place, it was now time to get a grown-up job. It all seemed so easy in those days, send off a few applications, and the likelihood was, that you would get offered all of them. I was offered a job as a marketing and events co-ordinator with a large IT company that I thought was way out of my league and skill set as it was advertised in the *Guardian*; I'm not sure why I was reading the *Guardian* in the first place but lucky I was. I thought I would give it a go as I had nothing to lose and could get another job if it didn't work out. I'm not sure if I was actually any good or if I just managed to bluff and bumble through all the things I didn't know, but I ended staying there for five and a half years, working on all their events. Big business here I come!

That was the start of the next eight years of corporate life for me and it was such a great experience. I met some lovely people, plus my career in travelling the world really took off. I was so lucky as I went to so many amazing places, firstly Europe including France, Germany, Italy, Sweden, Holland, Brussels; running events in each place. The people I travelled with were lovely, so we had some great times. We all got on well and it was during the 'boom' days where there seemed to be an abundance of money, so we travelled business class and ate in very expensive restaurants and stayed in amazing hotels. It's a shame how thing have changed!

The travelling then expanded to the USA where I went a few times. San Francisco mainly, as the head office was there, which was great as I got to know it quite well and it was very different working there and staying in five-star hotels from my budget holiday that I had spent there in my twelve dollar a night room with cockroaches! I love San Francisco—what a diverse and very friendly and interesting place. Over the Golden Gate Bridge is Sausalito which is just the most beautiful and quaint place with cherry blossom trees lining the roads, wooden houses and amazing seafood restaurants overlooking the water in abundance. A real must-do if you are ever visiting.

I stayed with the company for five and half years working in the same department and job which I never thought I would do, to be honest, until the company was bought out and I was made redundant. I was really sad at the time and remember going home in the middle of the day which felt very odd, sitting on my sofa not knowing what to do with myself. I can understand how this affects people that have worked in the same place for many years, with the same routine, going to the same desk and seeing the same people every day who then feel like the have no sense of belonging or use. But there are always new things out there to be discovered and fate always plays a part. In hindsight, this was probably the best thing to happen at that time as I was starting to get a bit restless and, sooner or later, I'm sure I would have left anyway.

I do believe that some things happen for a reason, except the really nasty stuff, of course, for which there is no explanation at all. Still, with my pick of the jobs available, my friend said there was a job going where she worked. The post was covering maternity leave in another large IT company working as an event manager. Following a couple of telephone interviews with the US bosses, I was offered the job! It was very full on and hard work, but I quite enjoyed it and it was at this company that I met Christina who became one of my closest friends for years to come, along with her fiancé, Hadi. Christina had quite a strong northern accent with a strong and capable personality and a wicked laugh! I'm so glad we became friends. My job, that was only supposed to be covering maternity leave, came and went and I ended up staying for over two years during which time the travelling increased and Europe became a large part of my travelling route, including one of my favourite places: Switzerland. I loved it so much that I went back on holidays to Geneva, Zurich, Luzern and Zermatt. They are all such stunning places and I'm sure there is much more for me to explore there.

Switzerland really does have it all: snow-capped mountains, crystal clear lakes, amazing countryside and an abundance of fresh air. There is always something going on and it's a great place for all types of sports. That, together with the old parts of the towns with cobbled streets in contrast to the new parts of town with shiny sleek buildings oozing obvious wealth, plus a never-ending choice of amazing restaurants and, of course lovely people, make it one of my favourite places. I absolutely love everywhere in Switzerland and dream to either live there, have a holiday home there or at least have lots of holidays there—what a luxury that would be. The location couldn't be better as it is so central and easy to hop on a plane to anywhere in Europe. Surely my French and German language skills would improve if I lived there!

With Cannes and Barcelona also becoming regular event locations for me as we held annual meetings and exhibitions in each city where we virtually took over the whole town and every hotel, I got to know each place quite well and I love both of them. Barcelona is fantastic as there is so much there: the beach, the old town again with cobbled streets and historic churches and the new town with amazing shopping, and intermittent tapas bars with *jambon* so delicious as it melts in your mouth. I once arranged a corporate party in *Casa Batlo*, the stunning Gaudi building which was magical as the delegates had drinks on the coloured tiled rooftop with the sun going down. One of my favourite restaurants in Barcelona is The Four Cats (Los Cuatro Gatos) which is hidden down a side alleyway that you would never come across just wandering around. As you first walk through the door, it looks like a small café, but once you are taken through a doorway and out to the back, the restaurant opens out into a spectacular galleried room where the orchestra play while everyone is enjoying a gastronomic experience. I would always request a table up on the narrow gallery, which is a bit rickety with uneven floorboards, but has a great view of all that is going on as well as the orchestra.

I have been so very, very lucky of which I am very aware of and very appreciative. I have been to places I would never have chosen for a holiday and seen things you don't often get to see.

During this time of corporate life and travelling around, I didn't have many serious boyfriends although, don't get me wrong, I had my fair share of dates and short-term relationships but I wasn't too bothered about settling down as I was having fun doing my own thing. However, it was at the weekends when I was on my own if my friends were busy that I did start to think about meeting 'the one' and settling down to a new chapter of my life. After all, it's not the same going to the cinema or out for dinner on your own and it's nice to have someone to share things with and make memories.

Introducing the lovely Christopher. I didn't meet my man until quite late in life—thirty-seven, in fact, but maybe that was a good thing as by then I knew what I wanted and had done my 'running around going out clubbing' thing. It took a while and a few dates with long periods of nothing in between for us to realise that we actually really liked each other and, since then, we were stuck together like glue.

We met on a blind date set up by my ex-boss, Lilly and initially, I wasn't too sure about going on a blind date and was quite sceptical. However, I actually knew of quite a few people that have met their long-term partners on blind dates so I guess it must work sometimes and if the middle man knows each individual quite well, they can see the similarities in interests or personalities so, in theory, should be a good match.

Christopher was a hairdresser and had many regular clients—one of whom was my ex-boss Lilly—and I'm sure like most visits to the hairdressers a good chat was had whenever she had her hair done. Lilly had cottoned onto the fact that Christopher was very sporty and one of his many sporting passions was waterskiing. She knew I waterskied and also enjoyed sports, plus as we were both single and looking to meet someone, it seemed like an ideal match.

Lilly was very excited and keen to tell me her plan to set us up on a blind date. It did take a few months to get organised as I had to wait until Lilly had her hair appointments to make arrangements. I was still a bit dubious and wondered if I should be doing it, but what did I have to lose? Our blind date venue was decided by me; a place that was busy with lots of people and somewhere that I could easily get home from if I needed to—always safety first.

We met at the train station. I felt like I should be carrying a copy of the *Times* and wearing a carnation for identification but it certainly wasn't like a romantic film as the station we met at was not in a desirable area, to say the least, so was actually a bit scary. Christopher had told me what colour shirt he would be wearing, which was dark purple, and as he was the only person at the station, he was easy to spot! I was contiuously staring at him—his features, his dress sense—all of which were good and he had the most amazing big smile.

We made polite introductions and headed towards town to find a bar where we drank and chatted and drank and drank and drank, due to nerves. We ended up in the cheesiest nightclub that you can imagine, surrounded by lots of people younger than ourselves. We even asked someone in the queue if we were too old to go in, to which he replied, "Oh no not at all, don't worry about being old as I'm really old at twenty-seven!" Rapidly heading for forty at that time, I don't think I will be going back anytime soon, if ever.

We did have a great time, but I think the alcohol took over towards the end of the evening. We both went our separate ways at the end of the night and that was that.

On Monday morning I was pounced on by Lilly who wanted to know all the details but was disappointed to hear that, "He wasn't really my type"; a phrase that she will continue to remind me of.

Occasionally Christopher and I texted each other but we both had busy social calendars so didn't arrange to meet up for quite a while until we agreed to meet for a coffee—no chance of beer goggles on this date, so it was a make or break.

I was waiting for Christopher outside a cafe in Windsor town centre: he was late. When he did finally arrive, he looked very nice indeed; his nice clothes and even nicer big welcoming smile. He did apologise for being late and said he couldn't park so all was good. We had coffee and got on really well. From that day onwards, we started to see each other and the rest, as they say, is history!

Lilly had been away travelling for a while and, to her surprise, when she came back, I told her the news that Christopher had cooked me dinner and we had started seeing each other. Christopher and I both saw Lilly quite often and she was still having her hair done by him so always reminded me of what I said after our blind date that was, "He was not really my type". Funny how things turn out!

Christopher is such a lovely person. He makes everyone laugh and is very kind, always looks lovely as he has an amazing dress sense, always smells lovely and I love him to bits. He never has a bad word to say about anyone and always manages to get the best out of everyone he talks to: something I can learn from there. He even told me once that, at school when he was chosen to be captain of the sports team, he picked all the kids for his team that were no good at sport to make them feel better and he was subsequently never asked to be captain again. How lovely was that! He is a diva on the dance floor and always the first to get up and have a boogie, much to all the ladies' delight as he is a very good mover!

He has one of those magnetic personalities that everyone is drawn to, and when he walks in a room, he has great presence. He has an abundance of energy which is sometimes slightly annoying as I don't and I am actually quite jealous of, and he is very into his sport. In fact, I think the only two sports that Christopher doesn't play are football and rugby, to my relief, and he will only watch the big matches on TV, as do I.

He has to try every sport going and gets annoyed if he isn't instantly good—tennis, windsurfing, running, going to the gym, waterskiing—his favourite though is snow skiing which he is incredibly good at. I always say his skis are like an extension of his feet as he is so at ease in them and glides down terrifying black runs making it look as if he is going for a walk in the park. Meanwhile, I am usually struggling to get up to the chairlift station, sliding backwards, getting my skis crossed over each other and trying not to poke anyone's eyes out with my poles as I wave them behind me trying to get my balance. You would never know I've been about six times but I just can't get the hang of it, much to Christopher's distress and somewhat disbelief that someone could be that useless at skiing, as he would love to go off-piste with me but I think this is just one of those things he will have to do without me. I think he has been skiing forty-eight times now and once skied with some Olympic skiers for fun, which shows his level.

I introduced Christopher to my friend, Fiona, and her husband, Bruce, and of course he hit it off with them both and could talk about skiing for ever with Bruce as it was their common interest. We went on a few ski holidays with them, which were brilliant as Bruce spoke fluent German he so took us to places we would never have gone by ourselves which I will never forget, and will always be grateful to them for taking us, but also great especially for Christopher, who now had someone of his standard to be able to just grab a map and go off skiing for miles over all terraineswith which he absolutely loved, while poor Fiona was stuck with me often taking my skis off and sliding down hills on my bum and being grumpy as I was scared! I'm sure she must have been bored stiff but was always so lovely and encouraging.

Christopher always said he would love to take blind or visually impaired people skiing but, as with everything, limited holiday time and money hold him back. What a shame and a waste for everyone as it would be fantastic for him, but more so it would give anyone with sight impairments or any other disability who wanted to give skiing a go an amazing experience.

When I first met Christopher, he lived in a very nice apartment about a forty-minute drive from me. It was a new duplex apartment so very 'shiny' and, with Christopher's good taste in furnishings and his clean and tidy ways (I call it his OCD but it's really not that bad!), it looked lovely. I had again set myself a deadline to move up the property ladder from my maisonette in Windsor. The deadline had arrived, so I was going to sell no matter what happened between Christopher and me. I sold my place and we decided that I could move into his apartment which was great; not so good for my commute in the mornings but you can put up with that when you meet someone lovely!

At that point in my life, well, actually it seemed to be the norm that I was travelling quite a lot and, one particular day, I had just got back from a trip so was having a lie-in in the morning as Christopher had left for work, when the doorbell went. As it wasn't my flat and I was being particularly lazy as I was tired from my trip, I ignored it thinking that they would come back if it was important.

I went back to sleep but, about fifteen minutes later, I heard a strange noise. At first, I thought it was the washing machine, but as Christopher dry cleaned all his clothes and never used the machine, I knew it couldn't have been that. The noise got louder and louder and when I heard a big crack, I knew there was something not right and someone was breaking in downstairs.

What would you do?

I think instinct took over and I want on to autopilot, scrambling to get dressed as quickly as possible. Without thinking, I flew down the stairs to the kitchen where the noise was coming from, to find a man halfway in the window!

I screamed at him. "Oi, what do you think you are doing?" Which was probably the most stupid thing to say as it was quite obvious! I told him that I had called the police, which was actually a lie at that point, as I hadn't had time. As the man was half in the window, I wasn't sure if he would back out or come in further, so I reached for my fruit bowl that was on the table ready to strike if he came towards me. Luckily, he was a complete coward so retreated and ran off, which was good for me as I love that fruit bowl which my sister brought back for me from France and it would have been irreplaceable and totally wasted on the idiot burglar's head!

I did then rapidly call the police who were very quick to come round and get the police helicopters up in the air looking for him as, apparently, he had recently come out of prison and had already committed other crimes including mugging an old lady—double coward. Unfortunately, they could not catch him, but I do hope and believe that one day he will get his comeuppance. As the saying goes, what goes around comes around.

Following that incident, and the fact that Christopher had already been broken into in the same flat before I knew him, he decided to sell it and that we would buy somewhere together.

My maisonette had sold quickly and easily due to its location (location, location, location as they say) but Christopher's was a bit more challenging as apartments were flooding the market at that time. Luckily, he eventually found a buyer and sold. After looking around for a while, we decided to buy in between our two old apartments and now have a lovely house in a very nice area near Windsor Great Park. It was interesting trying to fit in all the furniture that we had as we both seem to have a taste for oversized stuff and neither wanted to part with their own. Oh, the art of compromise, so we had his and hers sofas that didn't match! His, a brown leather massive manly-type thing and mine, a cream material squidgy thing which worked out well.

Our household is fairly typical and we have the usual set-up. I do the washing, food shopping, sort out all the bills and Christopher fixes, maintains and does all the 'boys' jobs' in the house such as unblock the drains, replace blown bulbs, fixes leaks, drills holes and vacuums the cars—great! He also does much of our interior design as he has such good taste. As per his dress sense, Christopher is very tidy which is very handy as I know that he will clean the parts of the house that I would probably not notice and leave to gather dust and grime, such as the windows, the oven, the corners of the kitchen floor and the plugholes—yuk.

Possibly the unusual thing about our relationship is that we do everything together. We go shopping together, we go to the gym together, we do the gardening together, we wash cars together (well I support by making the tea and a bit of hose holding as he does a much more thorough job of the cars than I do). Of course, we do see our own friends separately but not very often as most things we do as a couple which I like, although some may think it's a bit weird and possibly unhealthy for a relationship, but as we met late in life, we had a lot of time to make up for. We packed our time with having fun by doing sports every weekend without fail, including playing tennis, golf, waterskiing, running and swimming plus going to watch sporting events such as the golf at Wentworth, attending the Festival of Speed at Goodwood, going to Wimbledon and Queens for the tennis, the races at Ascot and many more which we did every summer.

Once we were settled in our new home together, I turned my attention to work and plucked up the courage to leave the stability, comfort, healthcare plan and not so nice office politics of my full-time job and decided to go self employed as a freelance event manager. My friend, Christina, stayed at the company but Christopher and I kept in touch with her and her fiancé, Hadi who got on like a house on fire with Christopher as they had the same silly but very funny sense of humour. I thought I would have enough contacts to get some work and if, after six months it was not working, then I would look for another permanent position, so I always had a plan B.

The first year was great. I didn't earn as much as I had been earning at my previous job but still enough to cover my half of our mortgage and bills. But what I did have was much less stress and quite a bit of free time that I loved and would go to the gym, go out running in Windsor Great Park amongst the deer and think to myself how lucky I was as everyone else was still travelling to the same place every day, stuck in a dark air-conditioned office from dawn till dusk.

The second year was, unfortunately, the beginning of the recession; it was a struggle and I had to take any jobs I could get. I've had a few great trips to the US working on events I like, but mostly working for people and events that I'm not so keen on but beggars can't be choosers and the mortgage had to be paid. I did think of getting another full-time job, but I wanted to give freelancing a fair go and was starting to enjoy the freedom of time off when I wanted.

My roles were varied; working for large event agencies, corporations and one-man bands that I knew from times of old, so I have been lucky with my contacts.

Working in an agency on short contract I was in desperate need of getting some more work booked in and I overheard someone in the office talking about a large job taking place in Africa and events staff were needed. I thought I would apply as I really needed to get some money coming in and, before I knew it, I had gone for the interview. The interviewers asked me where I would like to go in Africa, so Madagascar and Kenya were the first places that sprung to mind. How fantastic would that be as I am sure I would be placed in my preferred location and get some time off while I was there to explore. I was also asked where I would least like to go to, which I reeled off quite a long list that included Chad and the Congo, just because of the dangerous reputation they have. It had taken a couple of weeks to hear the decision. However, it was great news and I had been accepted to work in Africa. The not so good news was that the only role left as no one else wanted it was in *The Congo!*

Chapter Twelve
The Congo

The contract was working on one of many events launching a new mobile phone network that were taking place around the whole of Africa at the same time using live link-ups to bring them all together, which sounded exciting although we would be building the stage area from scratch in a field, which was interesting. I accepted the role with hesitation at being away for twenty-one days and also where I was going. My knowledge of the Congo was virtually zero; my only recollection of even the name was from that old TV advert for a fruit drink called Um Bongo! Oh dear, what had I let myself in for? As I looked into it further, the only news that I could find on the internet about Democratic Republic of the Congo were the bad bits about all the trouble and the war that ravaged the country.

I started to become a bit anxious, which rapidly turned into outright fear following our safety briefing with an external security company who could apparently, "Get us out", at a moment's notice if we dialled the emergency number. I had visions of SAS-style soldiers dressed from head to toe in blackout gear sliding down ropes from helicopters and plucking us out of danger and flying off to safety. I think I've been watching too many Bond films. We were also advised to buy a very thick rubber doorstop which I was initially confused about, however, it was explained that we should use this to wedge on the inside of our bedroom doors to stop anyone getting in!

I still went ahead, purely out of money desperation rather than travel curiosity, plus my friends, Christina and Hadi, said that if anything happened or I really wanted to come home, they would come and get me. How lovely and reassuring of them and I don't think they know how much that meant to me and still does. So I went… and I'm so glad I did as WOW what a place! It was an amazing experience and I had a great time, proving that you should always push yourself outside of your comfort zone as it really does broaden your horizons and you always look at things differently after you you have experienced something like that—in a positive way.

Even the journey out, travelling on my own, was an adventure. Changing planes for the final leg to Kinshasa was a real eye opener; no signs or announcements in the airport, just a person coming into the holding room and yelling which plane was ready to board. There were planes scattered all over the tarmac in no order or line, and people walking all over the runway. The most incredible and worrying thing was that the destination of each plane seems to be written on a piece of cardboard in marker pen and hung out of the pilot's window by a bit of rope Oh, my goodness—I had no idea if I was going to end up in the right place or not!

On arrival at Kinshasa airport, a colleague came to meet me; not difficult to spot as he would stick out like a sore thumb being the only white person at the airport apart from me! The scenes were like nothing I had ever seen as we embarked on the journey to our hotel. Colourful yellow and blue transit vans with their porthole-style windows cut out of the sides that looked like a tin opener had been used and wooden bench-style seating, which were used as taxis and raced around the roads.

Roadside stalls were selling all sorts of things, from food to the more unusual ones selling mounds of old tyres and one even displaying sets of hub caps fixed to tree trunks for every type of car available, although I have no idea where they got them from.

The most noticeable thing, though, was all the rubbish that lined the dirt roads. It was everywhere and every now and then we drove past a burning mound of rubbish as there was obviously no refuse collection as we know it. Everything is burnt including tyres, so the toxic smell really stuck in our throats. The rubbish burning would continue twenty-four/seven so there was never any let up in smoke and fumes. Plus, the toxins were going up into the atmosphere and into our bodies which made us slightly worried for not only our health but the health of the people living there; but in fairness what else are they to do with it?

My three colleagues and I were staying in one of only two hotels in the region and were told not to leave unless we were with our driver as it was too dangerous. Eeek. I did take some comfort from the airport-style X-ray machine at the entrance to the hotel which should have made us feel safe until we realised that no one bothered to check any bags when the alarm went off even when all the red lights were flashing. More worrying was when we saw that the back door of the hotel was permanently open offering a well-known back way in that bypassed the X-ray.

However, I'd spotted by far the most scary thing at this point which was the sign on the door of the hotel business centre where we were occasionally took our laptops down to do our emails on, that stated 'no guns allowed' which made me laugh in a hysterical sort of way.

Each day, we were driven to the office, not in a nice clean air-conditioned limo but in a pickup truck, taking it in turns to sit in the back of the truck in the open air, choking on dust and fumes from the burning rubbish and our stomachs left churning as we were bumped up and down over the massive potholes and rocks in the dirt road. Our driver, who doubled as our guide, was fantastic, he knew everything and everyone and, although he was of quite small frame and very young, we actually felt very safe with him.

It is amazing how quickly you adapt to your surroundings and get into a routine, we were starting to get braver and venturing out in the evenings, with our driver of course, and we found the most amazing restaurant near the UN building that was hidden by a high wall and barbed wire so you would never know it was there. It was kind of an ex-pat and UN employee oasis; very colonial with fantastic food that we were to visit regularly during our stay.

Surprisingly, the food and drink in DRC is extortionately expensive as everything has to be imported. Needless to say, I stuck to safe and plain so lots of rice which is always good for weight loss so that would be a bonus!

During my time in the Congo, I only really had one scary day which was when we went down to the port to meet a colleague who had travelled across the river from Brazzaville to help us with the project. As we parked up in our little white jute in the midday heat, we were quickly surrounded by people. Many of them were clearly high on either, drugs, alcohol or whatever else they could get their hands on, by the looks of their saucer-like eyes and the fact they couldn't stand up straight. Fights seemed to be breaking out all around us and there were some incredibly scary looking people around. One, in particular, who I think was an albino chap as he had white blonde hair and icy blue piercing eyes with a massive scar on his face and let's not forget the huge muscles he had, from looking after himself out on the street. I was keeping my eye on him, discretely of course, trying not to make eye contact while he staggered around as he looked as if he had nothing to lose and could suddenly decide to jump in the truck and steal the laptop I was unsuccessfully trying to hide. Luckily, our driver stepped in and managed to keep everyone at bay. Phew.

I was told I could either stay in the truck on my own while the others went to meet the boat or I could go with them. I decided safety in numbers was better even though it meant getting out. Our driver then introduced us to another man who had been hired as our fixer and guard while at the port and would look after us during the short walk from the car to the water's edge where we needed to meet our colleague from one of the many incoming boats. A bit overkill you may thing but, boy, I was glad he was there helping us.

Our guard was another one of the scariest looking people I have seen so I was very glad he was on our side. Very tall and pure solid muscle, again with a big scar on his face. He could obviously take care of himself and probably had had to at some point in the past. Looks can be deceiving and he was such a lovely and friendly guy and a lesson to us all to never judge a book by its cover.

As we started walking towards the water's edge, I stuck to this guy like glue trying to hide in his shadow to get through the crowds. The smells, the heat, and the noise; people bashing into you and staring as we were the only white people around.

We got to the jetty through a big iron gate that was being patrolled by the local police who were wielding very old AK47s, stopping anyone that tried to get through. You can't possibly imagine the chaos. Hundreds of people piling off the boats with no sense of order, all sorts of items being carried off in a great rush: flour carried in massive heavy sacks on people's heads that had leaked leaving the carriers with white hair and sweating profusely due to the heat; carpets and rugs in massive rolls; and sacks of food. I had to duck quickly as I saw the back of a rug swinging round towards my head and nearly knocking me over but this was no place to be getting in the way. The smell of diesel from the boats and big black plumes of smoke were choking and making me cough, but it was certainly an adventure!

I survived the port visit and the next day was a normal day going to the office. Well, as normal as it was in the DRC. As my bedroom in the hotel was five floors up, I jumped in the lift as I was meeting everyone in the lobby and I needed to call our driver to meet us at the front as he parked around the back of the hotel. But, oh, the lift started to shudder and then stopped completely. Luckily there were a few people in the lift with me who spoke English and we were all pressing all the lift buttons and discussing what to do. One guy had picked up the emergency phone which, unfortunately, seemed to not be connected to anything. It was a bit of a comedy moment. Everyone was keeping calm as it was getting hotter and hotter while we all frantically tried to get a signal on our mobiles. I managed to get a few bars by waving my mobile around so sent a text to my colleague who I hoped would see it. The text was read, and the alarm raised, so within half and hour we were all out. I was then promptly told off for being late; definitely a joke as I think my colleagues could see I had gone a bit white and was a bit shaky.

We were off to the field that had been identified to build our stage and hold the event. We shipped in satellites, lighting, power and everything to produce a high-tech event. The only thing missing was a toilet... basics we take for granted and, to my horror, one of the guys had started digging a hole in the ground and putting a curtain around it. No way. I would walk to a nearby cafe if I needed to, but hopefully as it was so hot and if I tried not to drink too much, I could wait until we got back.

One of our colleagues from the London office was coming over that day as one bit of vital kit had broken so he was bringing a replacement. I had asked our driver to go and collect him from the airport and get him through customs without any hassle and to make sure he had managed to get his luggage.

It got to mid-afternoon, and I saw our driver walking across the field towards me—on his own. Oh no, what had happened? Where was my colleague? It turned out that he hadn't travelled much, even in Europe, so was a bit inexperienced in the way to do things so had got into the first person's car who offered him a lift, not thinking to check that he was our driver. The next few hours were spent by our driver frantically calling around everyone he knew to track down our colleague as I was having a meltdown and thinking all sorts of awful scenarios, however, the many phone calls amazingly paid off and he was found and driven to our site.

Thankfully, after about three hours, I saw a figure walking across the field, in a full on thick grey business suit, leather shoes and clutching a large bag of very melted chocolate that he had kindly bought us from the airport. Ahh, bless him, he looked so pleased to see a familiar face and I think was a bit shaken by the whole episode so I doubt he will be doing any more travelling in the near future.

As I was far away from home, I made sure I managed to have at least a few phonecalls with Christopher but these had to be limited as it was so expensive. I was looking forward to the day's call as I'd been stuck in my hotel room all day working on the laptop and hadn't spoken to anyone, plus of course I was really missing him. As he picked up the phone, there was quite a lot of background noise, so I asked him where he was. To my surprise he was in the car, radio blaring, with his brother and his wife on their way to Lulworth Cove for a day trip on a lovely hot sunny English day. I was so jealous and really quite upset that I was not with them and was missing out on one of those fabulous events that create amazing memories forever. After I put the phone down, I vowed to go to Lulworth Cove with Christopher when I got back.

After a few weeks' work, the event date was finally upon us and, as usual with events, we were all tired and nervous about the event. Whether it would go well and if all the technology would work in the field, we had made into an event space. Luckily, everything went really well and the event was a success. When I think about how long we all worked so hard for planning the event and how much it cost, and all for a few hours to launch a product it was a bit of a relief that it was done.

I was now so excited and my packing to go home was frantic which didn't take very long as most of my clothes were going straight in the bin as they were so grubby and no amount of washing would get the ingrained dirt and smell out. Off to the airport—this was the best feeling ever—getting on the plane and knowing I was on my way home after a successful event, a topped-up bank balance and going back to see Christopher. I'd certainly worked hard for my money and could now enjoy a few weeks off at home spending twenty-four/seven with Christopher as I had missed him so much.

I have to say the Congo is the most fascinating and amazing place with lovely people and I am so glad that I grabbed the opportunity to go there with both hands and didn't let my preconceptions influence my decision to go as I would have missed out on a wonderful experience.

Chapter Thirteen
Just hit forty

For the next few months, I plodded on with different jobs and none as big or scary as the Congo. Time was flying past which it does when you are happy and busy until, one morning, I woke up to the realisation it was my fortieth birthday—aaaarrrghhhhh! My emotions are mixed. Happy, because it is my birthday and I should, in theory, be able to do whatever I like and everyone will be nice to me, bringing cards and gifts which would be wonderful. On the other hand, I'm a bit sad, as phrases that spring to mind are, 'the big four O', 'middle age', 'old', 'past it', and so on. As I look in the mirror to see the ever troublesome and rapidly expanding stripe of grey running down the middle of my head, and the increase of wrinkles around my eyes getting deeper by the day, I can't help but feel a bit depressed.

Oh well, life begins at forty so who cares? Who am I kidding? Reality bites. Conversations with my friends used to consist of fun nights out and planning lots of amazing holidays, what we were all doing at the weekends and that the prospect that our futures lives were so exciting. The world really was our oyster and we didn't seem to have a care in the world. Now, however, it is a different story as we talk about what type of mortgage everyone has, friends' children, money worries and how expensive the food shopping is, plus the various ailments that seem to be making an appearance and starting to seize up our bodies.

Suddenly and scarily, it dawns on me that I am running out of time. Life really is too short, so I need to get my act together and focus on doing all the things still left on my 'to do' list and actually get out there and do them instead of just thinking and talking about them; as I must admit I am a bit of a procrastinator…

However, already there are obstacles in the way. After a hard week's work plus cleaning, cooking, washing, ironing (although I have to admit I don't do that much…) and the numerous other general chores that we all have to do, along with trying to fit in some exercise to make sure I am fit, healthy and around long enough to actually do some exciting things, I am normally too tired to do very much at all and don't have any time left, as just living every day life just seems to get in the way!

In the run up to the 'big 4-0', I laughed off the ageist comments and didn't actually take too much notice. Everyone was asking if I was going to have a huge birthday party to celebrate, however, I've never been keen on being the centre of attention—hard to believe some of my friends would say—but I know I would spend the whole evening making sure everyone else was having a good time, not enjoying it myself. Also, I would hate to think that people would say I am only having a party to get presents which is weird as I certainly don't think that when other people have parties; one of my oddities or sensitivities, I guess.

No, my fortieth birthday celebrations were a bit different to most, as I opted for a subdued dinner at the local Italian with my family, consisting of my dad, step-mum, my sister and her husband, my step-sister and her husband, auntie and uncle and, of course, my boyfriend of nearly three years by this point, Christopher, plus the star of the show and birthday girl—me!

I chose the local Italian restaurant in the village as we can walk from the house. I'm getting lazy in my old age and can't be bothered to go very far or arrange taxis for everyone; keep it simple I say and, after all, it was my birthday so the one day I can choose what to do and where to go!

Now, our local restaurant is not your usual Italian. No crisp white linen, soft lighting and romantic background music, oh no. As you walk in the front door and take your coat off you are immediately greeted by the unmistakable sound of Frank Sinatra blasting out of the CD player and a wave of heat hits you as you are already halfway into the kitchen and standing in the middle of the restaurant as it is so small. You have to be very careful not to turn around too quickly or risk ending up on another diner's lap. Cosy is an appropriate word for the restaurant, with a compact main seating area that also houses the open kitchen so you can watch your food being cooked and the atmosphere is intimate, friendly and fun, all at the same time. The Parisian-style cafe tables (odd for an Italian restaurant), each have a candle on that is housed in an old wine bottle covered in rattan and a few weeks' worth of multicoloured candle wax that has dripped down the side and set solid. All are set very close together so there is always a high possibility of coming away with a burn hole in your clothes when squeezing past to get in or out of your seat; but that just adds to the fun. Pictures of the Rat Pack and Italian icons cover every inch of the walls and the smell of garlic and pasta fills the air. The manager, Roberto, is definitely a one-off and makes every night a serious party night with the guarantee of hysterical laughter, very strange dancing and a serious overdose of Limoncello which is not generally such a good idea but always seems to be at the time. Roberto is Italian, obviously, and with his spiky but longish dark hair, he has that cheeky boy quality that enables him to flirt with women of all ages in a splendid fashion which is highly entertaining and another reason the place is always packed. He doesn't leave the male customers out either as he knows everyone's name and is the friendliest and best host I have ever come across and always makes us laugh as he spins his way around the restaurant singing and clapping along to the music.

His best friend, Jonathan, whose parents have some sort of connection to the restaurant, arrives every Friday after work on his noisy 'cherry red' Harley Davidson to join the party. He is very flamboyant and a particularly striking looking chap, very tall and thin with blonde slicked back hair and a great dress sense, but who is also a ridiculously nice, genuine person.

We are always guaranteed a very warm and gushing welcome at any time. We once tried our luck by tapping on the door just before midnight following quite a few drinks elsewhere and, en route back home, realised we were hungry and even though they had just closed up, the door opened up to a big beaming smile followed by the kitchen reopening just to cook us dinner. That's what I call service and the benefit of living in a small village.

So, in hindsight, my idea of a quiet family dinner at the Italian may have been slightly foolish...

Ready for the big night. All my guests arrived at the same time, which is a bit of a squash as our front lounge is quite small with massive furniture, so everyone was crammed in like sardines as there is standing room only, with people spilling over in to the hall. I'd decided not to offer drinks as this would be a logistical nightmare in such a small space and I don't think there were enough glasses to go round, so I hastily ushered everyone out to start walking round to the restaurant in a big noisy huddle so no one got left behind. I was tottering along in my high heels as I'm not very good in heels due to weak ankles from previous and varied accidents, such as playing squash and the racing car accident, so I don't wear them very often even though my height, or lack of it, would suggest I should. I had a new flowery dress on and no coat as the evening is surprisingly warm and, with the lighter evenings really making an appearance, I was enjoying the fact that it was my birthday event and feeling full of the joys of spring.

As we arrived, Roberto came out to greet us with a beaming smile and open arms as usual and showed us to our long table that had been arranged especially for us in the middle of the restaurant.

We all sat down and, before we knew it, the wine has started to flow... and continued to flow to such an extent that even before we had looked at the menus, we had consumed quite a lot of both red and white wine, were all rather tipsy and had already started becoming a bit boisterous.

My Aunty Mo is great fun. She is a seventy-year-old version of Bet Lynch (a very old *Coronation Street* character for those who may not remember), with masses of blonde hair piled up on her head and chest that would give Bet a run for her money. Aunty Mo requested that Frank Sinatra stays put on the CD player, to which the ever-obliging Roberto agreed. As the volume went up our whole table started to sing, getting louder and louder as more and more alcohol was consumed, swaying from side to side and getting the other customers to join in and sing along with us. This soon turned into the whole restaurant getting up and dancing around the tables which is always entertaining as the risk of setting yourself alight increases, making the evening much funnier, especially after copious amounts of vino.

I'm sure we did have a great meal. However, I don't actually remember either ordering or eating any food which I'm sure some of you can relate to at one stage or another. As the evening went on, we continued singing and dancing until about midnight when we thought it was about time, we settled the bill and leave poor Roberto in peace to close up and go and lie down in a quiet, dark room.

We all fell out of the restaurant door onto the pavement and staggered back to my house, which I'm sure took twice as long as on the way there, probably due to walking sideways rather than in a straight line and probably annoying all the neighbours along the way. Funny how it is easier to walk in high heels after a few bottles of wine, maybe because you can't feel your feet? Back at home, it was time for tea so I sensibly put the kettle on, however, the oldies seemed to have other ideas. Aunty Mo decided that the lounge rug was in the way and had to go. I saw it flying out of the lounge door into the hallway as the sofas were also shoved out of the way against the walls to create a dance floor, albeit a very small one. The kitchen cupboards were raided and out came all the spirits including my best eight-year-old Havana dark rum, plus some of those old bottles at the back of the cupboard that have been brought back from holidays and contain weird looking plants floating around in them or are a radioactive green colour and that all taste revolting—you know the ones. The CD player was turned on and Frank was found in the CD rack so the dancing and singing could continue, getting louder and louder. Oh, our poor neighbours.

About two a.m. everyone seemed to be wilting slightly, so I took advantage of the lull and decided to call it a night. The taxis were called as everyone was staying in a local hotel, so Christopher and I stood outside the house to wave our guests off. As one of the taxis pulled up, Aunty Mo hadone more surprise in store to round off the evening and, in her tipsy state, proceeded to lift up her top and flash her chest at the taxi driver who I can only describe as past retirement age so he may have had a heart attack at any point. His face was an absolute picture and one of total shock, plus maybe a bit of pleasure! I don't think he was quite sure whether to just smile or rapidly drive off before the seventy-year-old blonde bombshell got in his car. It was absolutely hilarious and whoever said it is all downhill after you hit forty?

The morning after the night before, I woke up with an obviously hideous hangover—the type that used to last a few hours but now takes a week to shake off and another week to recover from the late night and severe lack of sleep. Why does that happen when you get older and is there an actual scientific explanation for it? Coupled with the reality that has firmly set in that I had now turned forty years old and there is no escaping that fact, or any way to turn the clock back, the new day did not start well. Maybe I was having a midlife crisis. I always thought it was funny when people said that and I thought it was just a saying, not actually a real feeling and definitely something that would never affect me as I can safely say that I have enjoyed every minute of my life so far and done everything I have wanted to do, except make money. Maybe this is why I was now having a major panic about running out of time? What should I be doing next and why do I seem to be more confused than ever?

When the big 4-0' comes calling, people react in different ways.

Some people have worked up to it since hitting thirty-five, planning what they will do on the big day; a massive party, a wild weekend away with the girls or nightclubbing as if you are still eighteen. However, some try to forget it but find it creeps up on them and takes them by surprise hitting them like a ton of bricks and resulting in major depression. Some people feel liberated as they have reached a stage where they no longer care what other people think; they have their own identity, are happy to grow old and grey gracefully and feel comfortable in their own skin.

Some try to defy it and use every modern convenience to look younger, whether it is wrinkle-busting face cream, hair dye and good make-up, maybe a bit of Botox here and there, or even full-on plastic surgery that will knock off a year or two. Some people feel that life really does begin at forty, but some sadly feel that they have already had the good years and it is all pipe and slippers from then on.

My feelings, however, are of panic at the realisation that I am running out of time to do all the things I want to with my life and also what lies ahead for me. I guess that's what they call a midlife crisis which I have to say I didn't enjoy and that seems to go on and on and on and I didn't quite know what to do to stop it, but at least I had the lovely Christopher by my side

Maybe it meant that I was not quite content with my achievements, so I started to think about what I have done with my life so far, what I still want to do, and if it will be possible to do everything, given time constraints, money constraints, work and all of life's additional challenges that it likes to throw up, all getting in the way. I wonder if I'm expecting too much from life and trying to pack too much in, or if I am not expecting enough of myself. Have I done enough so far or should I be doing more? After all, who needs sleep?

There is such a big difference in people at this age depending on how their paths have gone so far. Some look older for their age, some have kids and have already settled into middle age and are slowing down whereas some are still clinging on to their youth and getting out there. So should I give in to growing old, stay in on a Saturday night with my mug of cocoa on the sofa wearing my furry slippers and very unattractive tracky bottoms followed by an early night so I can get a good nine hours sleep? Should I let my hair go grey, dress in 'comfortable' clothes and sensible shoes and forget the latest make-up trends to hide those age spots and instead go with the *au naturel* look? Very tempting I must say, but I don't think I'm quite ready to give up to that extent; I would feel slightly lazy and don't actually want to look like a total mess the whole time for both me and Christopher.

Maybe I should try to maintain my youth and try to look younger, dress in the latest fashions, go for every trick in the book to look better and get glammed up every Friday and Saturday night in my LBD, getting out there and painting the town red with my girlfriends?

Unfortunately, some things are decided for you as it does seem to be a fact of life that, as I get older, I can't actually do the things that I used to do. I can't stay out until three a.m. every weekend any more, clubbing and drinking 'top rows' and 'tequila shots', being dared to eat the worm, as I'm tired by ten p.m. when most people are just going out and I now look for a chair to sit on rather than propping up the bar, which is a sure sign of age. The music is too loud, most of it I've never heard of and, in actual fact, I really don't enjoy that whole scene any more, especially the resulting week-long hangover that is no longer cured by a long lie-in and a bacon sarnie.

So, for now I am trying to get a happy medium. I do dye my hair, wear make-up, try to dress in fashionable clothes but in an elegant way so as not to look like mutton dressed a lamb and I do occasionally go out in my LBD which is now not so little; so more of a BBD (big black dress)! But I also enjoy my nights in on the sofa wearing my slippers and drinking cocoa. Hopefully this means I am growing old gracefully but not giving up the fight to look good, stay young at heart and still have pride in my appearance.

I'm sure you can relate to some or all of the thoughts that I had as a forty-something but I'm sure all agree that none of us should waste our time here and all of us should try and make the most of what we have to the best of our ability.

Chapter Fourteen
Life changer

Even though I was only away with work for up to a month, which in the grand scheme of things isn't a long time, it certainly felt like a lifetime and I can't tell you how amazing it always was to get back home. Everything once again familiar, sights, sounds, smells and, of course food. I had already lost some weight from being away on a few trips which was a bonus but I needed to get straight back into a proper fitness routine by going to the gym, running outside and waterskiing which always makes me feel better and would help to shed a few more pounds. I entered and ran the Windsor 8K race again for the second time; my time was shockingly bad and I'm not sharing it with you but at least I managed all the hills and crossed the finish line and, most importantly, I enjoyed it. I'm blaming my bad time on not enough training and the freezing cold icy rain that pelted me during the race, turning my legs that strange purple colour, and that's my excuse so I'm sticking to it!

I think everyone should join in one of the many charity walks, or runs that take place as it's always a great day with such a fun atmosphere, it's good exercise, you are helping a charity and you feel amazing when you have finished with all that fresh air in your lungs. What could be a better way to spend a few hours at the weekend?

The rest of that year passed with the normalities of life as Christopher and I plodded on and planned a trip to Prague at Christmas with my dad, Ellen, my sister and Arnold; what a great idea as I do find Christmas a bit boring at home with the whole three months prior building up to one day of eating and watching TV. I think it's really meant for the kids so any escape for me is good.

Uunfortunately, holidays were not as frequent as they once were and usually when deciding where to go and how much luxury we can afford, a discussion about needing to replace the broken fridge or the leaky guttering always takes place. Our house is still in need of lots of redecoration and seems to be like the Forth bridge as repairs are never-ending. Sadly, the winning argument of spending money on holiday or house usually goes to house but that is OK as it is nice to have a lovely home to come back to; as the saying goes, an Englishman's home is his castle but, in this instance, there was no competition and the holiday won.

Just prior to Christmas, Christopher and I were getting ready for bed as usual one night and, while cleaning our teeth in the bathroom, I noticed one of the moles on Christopher's back looked a bit strange. He has a lot of moles and we joked about what picture would emerge if we drew a dot to dot on his back, however, I made him go to the doctor's just to be on the safe side and get it checked out. He had actually previously asked about this mole and it was dismissed as being OK, but I wasn't convinced.

I went along with him this time and we were again told that everything looked OK, however, I was not happy and stood my ground until it was agreed for the mole to be removed, although under duress, and was noted down as for 'cosmetic' reasons. I can certainly see how people slip through the net and are fobbed off, which shouldn't happen. The procedure was done at the doctor's surgery which didn't take long and few weeks later and all was well.

Off we all went to Prague for Christmas; how lovely all of us being together going on holiday. On Christmas Day, we all went to the Christmas market, wandering around looking at all the stalls selling gingerbread, gifts and local food and drinks. We decided to have some mulled wine—obviously just to keep us warm—when it started to snow: perfect timing! Everything looked beautiful as the snow started to cover the ground and we were all together having a lovely time although, gosh, I've never been so cold in my entire life and I had so many clothes on it was hard to move my arms!

Prague is a beautiful place; cobbled streets, medieval buildings and little cosy bars tucked away from the main tourist attractions. We all went out one evening for something to eat and, then on the way back, piled into a bar for a last drink before returning to our hotel. Well, that was the plan anyway, however, it turned into one of those nights to remember!

The bar was a Cuban bar and from the outside just looked like a small café, however, when we got inside, the salsa music was pumping, and there were amazing floor to ceiling paintings of Cuba covering the walls. Of course, it turned out that the owners were amazing salsa dancers and had previously won awards for their dancing, so now taught others. As the evening went on and the drinks were flowing, everyone was getting up to dance, being taught salsa moves and given instruments to play—what fun! Much later on in the evening, and when only the hard-core guests were still there which included us, my dad and Ellen and a handful of customers, the owners opened up some doors and, to my amazement, there was a huge wooden staircase leading down to a massive nightclub-style dance floor and stage. We all piled downstairs and carried on dancing—my dad drinking absinth which looked like green mouthwash and my sister smoking a huge Cuban cigar! Very surreal!

We had such a great time and it made that particular Christmas a really special one with some great memories.

On our return from Prague, we all got back to normal and Christopher had to go back to work before New Year, however, I was lucky enough to have the whole week off. One morning while I was just pottering around and doing the washing, the phone rang. It was our doctor with the results of the mole biopsy. Christopher had a malignant melanoma—skin cancer.

I couldn't quite take it in. It felt like a ton weight had been dropped on us and our whole lives were about to change although I don't think we realised to what extent or how serious it was.

Here started our journey of numerous trips to London to the hospital and a number of operations that is hard to imagine; navigating our way around the NHS, trying to work out the best thing to do, as trust me, you are not always given all the options or information so you need to do your own research in order to know the right questions to ask. We often came home more confused than before we went so, after a while of the feeling of being baffled and only being offered the standard procedures, I decided the only way was to get clued up and get tough. During the next visit I took out my long list of questions that we wanted answering but, as usual, these were not getting answered. I decided to stand my ground and demanded that someone in authority speak with us before I would leave the room, which did the job, and only then did we start getting the answers we needed. This was only one hospital, under pressure as they all are, plus they were not specialists in cancer, which didn't help our case.

Poor Christopher, he was subjected to so many horrendous operations.

We had to go back into London for the results of the moles that were sent off and analysed, which we were obviously very nervous about. We often had to sit in the depressing waiting room—well, more like a corridor—looking at the wall and with people treading on you to get past, for two or three hours each time. We were finally called in, sat down and the surgeon looked at us with a very steely face and said, "Good and bad". My heart sank and I can only imagine what Christopher was thinking.

We were well and truly in the system and still at the beginning of this horiffic journey. Another major operation was planned which was truly horrendous and made even worse, if that were at all possible, with Christopher being kicked out of hospital on the same day. He was brought round from the anaesthetic and was in so much pain he could not move. He was made to stand up and nearly collapsed and told that he would have to leave as the staff all stood round with their coats on waiting to go home. We live about an hour's drive from the hospital and that night it was very heavy snow. Quite unbelievable. I don't know how we got home and it was one of the worst nights of my life, or so I thought at the time, and it shouldn't have even mattered how bad it was for me as it was much worse for Christopher.

I couldn't see the road for the heavy snow falling, I was scared that we were going to crash and every bump in the road was agony for Christopher who had to sit with his head in a bowl in the car all the way home as

172

he felt so sick. I know it is not all the fault of the staff at the hospital, but I do think that patients should not be kicked out when they are so ill. Then the icing on the cake was that we had to wait three agonising weeks for results.

While Christopher was recovering, a few complications arose that we had to deal with: swelling, infection, the usual stuff. Fiona, my friend, was her ever thoughtful self and sent over cooked dinners so we wouldn't have to worry about shopping and cooking. She even sent a bottle of wine which was so kind of her and gratefully received. That is what you call a really good friend.

Recovery was going well and Christopher was desperate to get back to some sort of normality, so we started to go running in Windsor Great Park as I had again signed up for the Windsor 8K. No one would have ever known Christopher was ill as he just kept pushing through to do his sports and never ever moaned. We set out on a longish run to get some training in and decided to take a different route to normal to extend the mileage. Now, he knew my sense of direction wasn't the best and I did say to him, "don't go off without me", however, it seemed to fall on deaf ears as I watched the back of him disappear around a corner. I thought I knew where I was going and tried to follow him although I could not see him any more. Of course, this ended up in me getting lost and my 'longish' run ending up being eleven miles which definitely was not the plan. I had called

Christopher after about nine miles, in serious agony and annoyed at having been abandoned. He asked one of the park wardens to come and find me, which was so embarrassing, so when he drove up to me I pretended to be fine and declined a lift back. Christopher did eventually come and rescue me and I hobbled back with him but it was obviously all his fault and I didn't speak to him all the way back to the house.

Yes, most definitely back to normal.

Christmas and New Year came and went again—I hoped the coming years would be better than the one that had just gone with no illnesses, an abundance of well-paid work, hopefully a couple of holidays and definitely lots of fun along the way.

Some work did pop up fairly soon—a couple of months in Qatar with one of the big event agencies. Great for the experience and even better for the bank balance but I was definitely not keen on being away for that long. However, needs must, and I really did need the money as per usual so, once again, into the unknown I went with plans for lots of lovely things for Christopher and I when I got back already in place so we had something to look forward to.

Chapter Fifteen
Qatar

The time came to head off once again on another work trip and I was so sad when I left and kept crying as I didn't want to go and leave Christopher, but I had to. Once in the taxi I knew I just had to focus on getting the job done and, as it would be so busy, hopefully the time would pass really quickly.

What an arrival—wow—again. After a long flight with my colleagues, we were greeted by the most amazing blue sky and the first thing I noticed was how hot and sticky it was. In the taxi from the airport to the apartment that we were to be staying in, we were overtaken by virtually everyone as they sped past in their huge four-wheel drives, throwing up loads of dust and sand in our path making it tricky for our driver to see the road ahead which was slightly nerve-racking. The roads all looked the same to me, all long and straight, sandy and lined with similar looking buildings on both sides, so the only way to navigate your actual whereabouts is by the different decoration on each of the roundabouts or the landmark of a new skyscraper in the distance. We first passed through the older areas with their Moroccan-style buildings—the only way I can think of to describe them but which is probably totally incorrect, and possibly even offensive, for which I apologise! We then turned the corner to see Al Corniche which was the road that swept around the sea in a horseshoe shape lined by a wide pathway where families walk together; the men in their gleaming white thobes and the women with their heads and faces covered with only their storytelling eyes on show that have been made up with thick black eyeliner, all enjoying the hustle and bustle of the waterfront. In the distance I could see many tall sleek glass buildings as we headed towards the new town where our apartment would be. There are so many new skyscrapers in Doha that all have the most fantastic views as you are up in the clouds. Hotels, office blocks and apartments all stood together, just like New York—quite breathtaking.

I would describe Qatar as Dubai ten years ago, and hope I don't offend anyone again with my description as it is meant in a nice way. The buildings are going up quickly and tourist attractions are being built. The Pearl, with its marina and high-end shops, makes a lovely place to sit and drink coffee and watch the world go by while drooling over the multimillion-pound boats— long and sleek with tinted windows, I can only ever dream of setting foot on one let alone owning one. The Museum of Modern Art is a beautiful place to visit. It's a large imposing building of lightly coloured stone with a background of turquoise water that glistens in the sun. As you walk inside, the sheer height of the ceiling makes you glance up and beckons you to walk up the staircase which is stood elegantly in the middle. The pearl exhibition was on during my visit which was fascinating and educational—I now know which type I would like to buy, or be bought!

Back in the old part of town, the souk with its narrow paths that you could easily get lost in was a great place to wander around at night when it is at the height of hustle and bustle as everyone ventures outside in the cooler evening. The shopkeepers love to barter with you for their wares; scarves, rugs and spice shops are all on offer and as you shop, the smell of sweet incense fills the hot evening air. At the weekend this is the place to be as there is all manner of entertainment taking place in the main square to sit and watch while sipping the favourite local drink: lemon and sugar.

I was with a fantastic small group of people who all wanted to see and do as much as possible after work, so I enjoyed some great days out while I was there and, with Saturday being a work day in the Middle East, my first day off was a Sunday when the camel racing took place. Although it was a ridiculously early start to avoid the midday heat, the whole thing was so funny and I didn't stop laughing. All the camels raced around the track—just like a horse racetrack—but with their long lanky legs flailing all over the place, mouths frothing and the chaos of the locals trying to keep up in their four-wheel drives around the outside of the track to follow their own camel, which unavoidably turns into a

177

right old dusty bun fight! They use small robots on the camels' backs for jockeys instead of heavy people, so no cruelty to the camel, which I was very relieved to see. What fun and definitely something that I had never seen before!

The sporting calendar in Qatar was in full flow while I was there so I was lucky enough to be able experience the Tour de Qatar which was amazing—the cyclists whizz past so fast that if you blink you miss them, but an amazing sight all the same. The Masters golf was being held at the Qatar Golf Club which is a very splendid place and I was lucky enough to be given a ticket to go as our contacts knew I was keen. Seemingly golf is not as popular as it is in Europe and the USA, so I was able to stand right next to the players while they teed off and walk around the course with them virtually alone. Lastly, to Christopher's envy, while I was checking out some conference space at the local motor racing circuit, I got a call through on my radio to say that the high end Drivers' Club event that was taking place had a spare thrill ride slot. Well, I am definitely not one for speed, however, the opportunity had presented itself to me and it would have been a crime to have turned the offer down. Off I went, heart in my mouth and got into the most beautiful Porsche Panamera to be greeted by the beaming smile of the driver who was a very well-known rally driving champion which I was not aware of. Oh dear. The wheels spun and off we screeched. I screamed instantly as I felt as though we had sped off at nought to one hundred in just a few seconds, only to be told that we hadn't even left the pit lane so in actual fact weren't going very fast at all. This, of course, fuelled the driver's amusement as he drove even faster, sideways, around the track with me screaming that I didn't want to die, but he was very good and kept checking that I was OK and hadn't passed out. I have to say that this was the scariest thing I've ever done and, at one point, I actually felt my eyes rolling around in my head like you see in the *Tom and Jerry* cartoons. Relieved to finally have my feet back on solid ground, albeit with my knees shaking so I couldn't walk for a while, I was so pleased to have been given the opportunity and pleased with myself for having accepted and adhered to my own motto in life which is to try everything once even if you never want to do it again, which I most definitely didn't.

I am sure you are thinking I was on a big jolly, but we did work really hard and it wasn't nice being away for that long. I don't normally get homesick but I did in Qatar; it's the most horrible feeling not being where you want to be and who you want to be with.

Luckily for me, there seemed to be an abundance of gyms in the apartment blocks and hotels to keep me busy and my mind occupied, so I was also able to get quite fit while I was there as my colleagues and I encouraged each other go each day after work as we all wanted to shed a few pounds. While I was feeling so fit, mistakenly thinking I would keep up the routine when I got home, I madly signed both myself and Christopher up for the Windsor half marathon—possibly a bit ambitious on my part but I would give it my best shot even though the hills may finish me off.

Two months passed slowly but, finally, it was time to go home, thank goodness. Back from Qatar I was so pleased to be home and vowed never to go away for that long ever again. I luckily managed to get a short contract working as a campaign manager for a candidate running in the local elections, which meant no travel, and then work at a hedge fund conference which was in London. However, once again, I was then searching for work so my hopes for a fruitful year seemed to be fading as the year seemed tougher than the last on the work front. Things were starting to drop off and go wrong with my car which really needed replacing, so my already depleted savings that doubled as my future pension needed to be delved into once again, leaving not much in the pot. However, I was definitely making the most of the time I had at home enjoying the house and garden in the sunshine and of course being with Christopher. Oh,, how it was good to be home.

I was definitely starting to feel my age; I love our house and spending time pottering garden and moaning about neighbours' loud music. I've turned into a grumpy old woman! I actually hated going away and enjoyed staying around the house just doing nomal stuff, cleaning, looking after the house and watching the birds in the garden. Is that what happens when you get older? Am I destined to be a complete hermit by the time I reach seventy?

I love the birds. I am not a full blown 'twitcher' but could sit and watch the birds on the feeders all day every day and never get bored as they are so cute and all have their individual personalities. We are lucky enough to be visited by a wide variety of birds—all types of finches, blue tits, blackbirds, robins, green parakeets and even a woodpecker!

Outside the kitchen window there is a lovely tree in the garden that has purple flowers in the summer. Underneath sits a bird table that my dad made, with an adjustable roof that is set to low to stop the pigeons getting in and gobbling all the food up! There are two hanging feeders on the stand and underneath is a bird bath. Across the back of garden, on the fence, is a bird box, also made by my dad (he is very clever), that usually has blue tits nesting in. At the side of the garden is the garage which is covered in foliage including clematis and passion flowers that the birds love, especially the blackbirds that nest in it yearly. If I'm at home, I am usually on 'bird watch' to ensure all the baby birds fledge OK and aren't eaten by next door's cat that I often threaten with the hose if I see it creeping in to the garden. One year, a baby blackbird plopped out from the foliage into the middle of the grass and sat there looking like a big fluff ball, just waiting to be eaten. I spent days following it around to make sure it survived and luckily it did!

This may all sound lovely, however, the reality is that I do have to go to work and earn money and have at least another twenty years of work ahead of me. I'm not a lazy person but I would be more than happy working at the local dogs' home, taking them for walks every day with no stress or travel, however, given the size of our mortgage, bills and general living expenses I don't think that would work unfortunately; which I'm sure a lot of people can relate to.

Chapter Sixteen
Home for good

Finally, at forty-two and after being together for five years, Christopher asked me to marry him! I kind of knew it was coming as we had talked about it, but it was still very romantic.

It was early one Saturday evening in midsummer when we walked into Windsor Great Park taking a bottle of chilled champagne and some plastic glasses with us for a liquid picnic. It had been a very hot day and was one of those rare balmy summer evenings that I long for all year round and can't get enough of. We wandered up to Cow Pond—the lily pond—that was covered in the most amazing vibrant pink and yellow flowers and looked stunning. There was an old bench on one side of the pond so we sat down and took in the last of the sunshine that was glistening on the pond, while watching the ducklings swimming around—idyllic as there was no one else there so it was like having our own private, very grand garden! Out came the champagne from the rucksack and we sat sipping our drinks enjoying the wonders of nature. Christopher was looking nervous and then, all of a sudden, hastily got down on one knee and asked me if I would marry him.

Of course, I said yes and instantly started crying. A couple then appeared with their dog who we announced our news to, which made the lady cry!

The ring was beautiful, a platinum solitaire that Christopher had had made especially for me, so unique and it matched a pair of earrings he bought me when we first met.

We decided to get married the following June giving us time to save some money and do the planning. Arranging the wedding was easy for me being an event manager. I am not being big-headed but I manage logistics every day so I knew what needed doing and, although I don't arrange weddings, it was a bit like being at work but obviously a lot more fun. Having looked at a few options of where to get married, that included getting married outside somewhere in the Great Park amongst the trees with the birds singing, or in a building overlooking the polo fields, two of our best friends, Christina and Hadi, and their young son, Sebastian, who lived not far from us and who were a constant support during all the dark times, suggested that Wentworth Golf Club may not be as expensive as we thought and very posh!

I wanted everything in one place so none of our guests had to drive anywhere and, as Wentworth was only five minutes down the road from our house, plus with the obvious glamour of the place, it ticked all the boxes.

We booked the date; a Rat Pack tribute band to entertain our guests while sipping a carefully chosen selection of cocktails out of old-fashioned glasses; the amazing three-tier white chocolate iced sponge cake; sorted the food menu; and, of course, I had a field day looking for a wedding dress.

Having sent all the invitations out, we started to really look forward to our special day, however, it was not to be.

All was going so well, however, a couple of months later, following a routine check-up, we had yet more bad news about Christopher's health as the cancer had returned. We had to cancel the wedding as he would need to go into hospital for surgery to have more lymph nodes removed.

It was so awful for him. Not only was the operation horrendous with tubes and drains sticking out of him, so was the fact that it had returned when we finally thought it had gone away.

We wanted to get the surgery done as quickly as possible, to just get it done, but had to wait for a while which was agonising and gave us more thinking time, which is the worst thing in that situation. The date arrived and Christopher had the surgery, which was pretty traumatic. During his recovery time, there were many challenges with infections and swellings which we dealt with one by one and, after a while and a lot of sheer determination, defiance, willpower and positive attitude, once again Christopher got back on his feet and surprisingly quickly; so we were able to once again think about the wedding.

Amazingly, there had been a Saturday cancellation at Wentworth, and we were able to rebook our wedding in the same place; even in the same room, just a different date, so I think it was fate. They were so helpful and understanding and helped us reorganise our day.

We did have to scale everything down as money was now tight, having both had so much time off work, so the guest list was reduced to twenty-five from fifty, the Rat Pack were cancelled and, although my dress came off the shelf from a department store, it was still the most beautiful dress I had seen. It was a shame that we couldn't invite all the people we wanted to, however, the day was a lovely intimate affair. Christopher's boss came to the house and did my hair for me while we were sipping champagne and my sister was there helping calm my nerves as the whole morning was a bit surreal in an exciting sort of way. Luckily, the heavy rain that had fallen for the whole of the previous day and night, stopped just before I was due to leave the house and the sun came out, showing the clearest, bluest sky and warming everything up. My dad picked me up and drove me to the venue, which is generally filled with large expensive cars which my dad parked next to in his very small economy 'Postman Pat' car as we call it. The ceremony was emotional—well, on my part anyway. As my dad walked me to the room, I was managing to hold it together until we were just a few steps away from the door when one of the cloakroom ladies at the club said how beautiful I looked. It all went pear-shaped from that moment as I crumbled and couldn't stop crying. I made poor Christopher wait for about ten minutes wondering if I was ever going to arrive and his nervous energy apparently kicked in as he was at the front of the room entertaining all the guests! I walked in to see Christopher's gorgeous smile and walked towards him. I blubbed my way through the entire service, which I really didn't think I would do, only just managing to get my words out, but then relaxed and, after the ceremony had finished, we all spent the day out on the large terrace overlooking the pool in the warm sunshine enjoying our day with family and friends, an abundance of nicely chilled champagne and fabulous food. Our wedding day could not have been more perfect.

As Christopher was still not quite on top form and we were now broke, our honeymoon was not a lavish fortnight in an exotic paradise but a few days at Lulworth Cove. I had wanted to go with him since missing out when I was away in the Congo and he had gone there for a day trip with his brother. It was a long drive and for most of the time it rained and was rather chilly, but we did get one really lovely day and I remember us sitting outside on our terrace overlooking the cove, warm sun shining down, while we watched Wimbledon, eating some strawberries we had bought and sipping yet more champagne that we had taken with us—just perfect.

Back home and quickly back to normal but now, as a married couple, we seemed to move into a phase of ongoing and constant battles with Christopher's health as the cancer seemed to be an aggressive one. He had more and more operations and I think we lost count, or decided to stop counting after seventeen, but as we once again waited for more agonising results, we knew he would have to go back in for another big operation. It was seeming as though we would never really be free of this horrendous illness, as it was ongoing, we just had to learn to live with it, with the highs and lows which were devastating and wearing on both of us, but I just can't imagine how utterly terrifying it was for Christopher. I wish there was something I could do as feeling completely helpless is another common emotion and I would have taken his place in a heartbeat.

The trips to the hospital were becoming more regular with never-ending tests, but the waiting was the worst thing; not knowing if it had got worse, or what news we would be given every time we went in.

Christopher still pretended to feel OK and wanted to do normal stuff, so we tried to carry on as we always had done.

We went away for a long weekend to Scotland as one of Chrisophers clients had a holiday home on the shores of Loch Lomond and offered it to us for a few days which was so lovely of them.

It was a great distraction as we were out in the fresh air looking at beautiful scenery, playing golf, going on boat trips and even on a sea plane which was a highlight for Christopher, but always with other things in the back of our minds.

Chapter Seventeen
Iceland together

With all these bad things happening and another year having passed, we decided to try and do yet more normal things which was really important for our mental wellbeing. So, to cheer ourselves up, we decided to go away for Christmas to somewhere we have both always wanted to go—Iceland! Christopher was feeling OK, or so he said, and, although we couldn't really afford it, we decided to have a nice treat, live for the moment and manage the overdraft later.

How exciting! It was only going to be a flying visit—two and a half days in Iceland but we planned to pack a lot in. I got a bit carried away and bought some snow grips for my boots—kind of like chains for car tyres but for shoes—which Christopher thought ridiculous and kept laughing at me. However, as I slip over when it's raining, let alone snowing, I thought the grips would be very practical. I also invested in a head torch—not sure why but it made me feel like an explorer and I thought it may be useful given there was only about four hours of daylight expected each day.

As we flew into Iceland on Christmas Eve evening, all we could see was white. Snow, snow and more snow.

We had arrived in blizzard conditions with the snow being blasted sideways along with the plane, which was slightly worrying!

We got on the coach and hung on as it slid around the bends in the road. I guess the Icelanders are used to it and Christopher thought it was great fun, but I was a bit nervous I must admit.

Even though it was dark, we could see how much snow there was: metres of the stuff and it was still coming. Christopher was like a small child as he loves the snow so was overexcited and hyperactive for the whole journey.

We finally reached the town having dropped a few people off at other hotels. I always get a bit apprehensive when you see people left at hotels in remote locations and hope the brochure was truthful in its description of a 'central location'. Luckily it was and, as we pulled up to our hotel, it looked warm and cosy with lights around the windows inviting us in. An amazing building with massive windows and really high ceilings—phew!

A quick drink in the bar with its cowhide sofa covers (fake, I'm sure, well at least, I hope), as we wanted to get up early so as not to waste any of our time there.

We awoke the next morning—Christmas Day—to more snow. We exchanged cards and a few small presents that we had taken with us and, after a quick breakfast, we got ourselves ready for the first excursion of our short holiday which was a trip to the Blue Lagoon thermal pools which, yes you are correct, are outside!

My goodness, it was cold. I had my ski clothes on plus quite a few layers, hat, gloves, scarf and very thick socks but wasn't prepared for the fact that once we were at the pools, there was a short distance outside that we had to navigate to get from the changing rooms to the pool in only swimwear and flip-flops. My feet went instantly bright red and then a bit blue as I hurried to the pool trying not to slip over in front of everyone in my flip-flops on the icy path.

Christopher was having a ball as he loves extremes so was revelling in the fact that it was minus ten degrees and he was in his swimming shorts. Hard man or mad man but, whichever, he was having fun which was the main thing.

The water was such an amazing colour—piercing turquoise—with steam coming off it and a swim up bar sat right in the middle.

We got in and swam around for a while, the hot thermals making some parts of the pool so hot that I couldn't put my feet down. There was a section that had a wall of mud at the side which you could paste on your face and was supposed to be beneficial for your complexion, so we covered ourselves before going into the natural steam room built into the cliff, which was amazing.

We came out of the steam cave, washed off our mud packs and headed over to the bar to get a drink, probably undoing all the healing powers of the water and mud.

It was the best Christmas Day ever; standing in the middle of the hot Blue Lagoon pool, freezing cold ice and snow surrounding us, sipping a cold beer. As we said cheers and wished each other a Happy Christmas it started to hail. Golf ball-sized ice balls started to hit us so we had to take shelter; it was so funny and a now a great memory of a fantastic day.

That night we had booked a restaurant for Christmas dinner so enjoyed lots of lovely food and wine surrounded by the restaurant decor of candles, fairy lights and, of course, a Christmas tree. What a great end to a wonderful Christmas Day.

On Boxing Day, we were up even earlier as we had two excursions booked in! The first was a glacier walk plus ice wall climbing—fab! I have always wanted to try ice wall climbing but never managed to do it, but here was my opportunity and I was really excited, with a tinge of nervousness.

The snow was still falling and had not stopped since we arrived so was getting deeper and deeper. We were collected by the tour company in the pitch black and taken to the central meeting point where we saw our transport for the day; how brilliant as it was a monster truck! We met our guide and headed off on the long drive to the glacier, the first hurdle being actually getting into the truck as my shortfall in height was not well suited to the massive trucks that were very high off the ground. They had the most massive wheels and tyres I have ever seen and, as we sped off, I quietly screamed to myself as I knew I was going to be petrified for the whole day. Of course, Christopher was loving the experience and beaming from ear to ear.

After a few hours of driving, we finally arrived at the bottom of the glacier where our group were given a safety briefing, safety helmets, harnesses and ropes and crampons to wear. The blizzard was getting worse so we were told not to stray one inch from the guide's footprints as visibility was very low and crevasses had been covered up by snow, so we could easily disappear down one. Now I was really worried.

As we started to climb, we quickly got used to the crampons, although it was hard going at the bottom as there were lots of rocks and I found it difficult to keep up the pace with the thick snow and my short legs.

We all looked like Scott of the Antarctic with our faces covered with our scarves to stop us getting frostbitten faces from the icy wind, and some, including us, wearing our ski goggles.

At certain points on the way up, we would all gather round the guide, ensuring we stood exactly where we were told, for him to then show us that we were standing a few feet from a crevasse that he had seen a few days earlier before the snowfall. He was so knowledgeable, thankfully, and took us the safe route to the top of the glacier, through ice holes and ice caves, explaining the formation and layers of the ice with all its different shades of white and blue—it was wonderful and so interesting.

It was finally time for the ice wall climbing and I was very excited, only to be told at the last minute that, unfortunately due to the weather closing in, the ice climbing had to be cancelled. Such a shame. I was very disappointed but secretly a tiny bit relieved as it was hard enough to stand still in the wind and snowstorm, let alone climb up an icy wall!

It wasn't until we had got back down to the bottom that Christopher told me that my helmet had been wonky on my head for the whole day and that I looked like the village idiot. Nice of him to let me walk around like that before telling me, but very funny.

Christopher managed to take the most amazing photo of me on his phone, through an ice cave—it really was so incredible I would encourage everyone to go.

Time on the glacier was running out as we had to get back to the bottom before it got dark and back to the hotel for our second excursion in the evening which was to go and see the magical Northern Lights!

Again, we were collected from our hotel and this time the monster truck was even larger; really, I didn't know they could be made that big! Christopher hoisted me up into the truck where there were four other people sat in the back, all coming with us to see the lights.

It was a hilarious night. There were seven monster trucks, all of us in convoy, 'chasing' the lights. All of the trucks were connected by radio, so the drivers were talking to each other as the updates from control came in about the weather and where we were most likely to see the lights. It was great fun as we rapidly and frequently changed direction speeding along the roads to catch a glimpse of this magnificent sight and wonder of nature.

After about three hours of chasing the lights and a few stops to try and see them, we made our last stop in the middle of nowhere to all get out and take a look. I jumped down from the truck and promptly sank up to my thighs in snow so had to be rescued by Christopher. We all stood around in silence, watching the sky and holding our breath in anticipation.

Every now and again, the guide would shout and point up to the sky at a very dim glow that could have been from the street lights in the distance, but we like to think it was the Northern Lights, even if it was just for a second.

On the way back, we were all a bit disappointed, but the guide told great stories of trolls for the whole journey and was so funny that he kept us all entertained.

It is said that you are lucky if you see the Northern Lights. Maybe one day.

My head torch had turned out to be a really great idea for this trip and perfect for this nighttime outing. Unfortunately, due to our rush, I forgot to take it with me so it never got used.

Chapter Eighteen
The worst year ever

I am well aware that time is very precious and I always made sure that I packed Christopher's and my every moment with lovely fun things when times were 'normal'. Unfortunately, money does make the world go round and you need a certain amount of it to do a lot of the things you want to do in life.

My personal list of fun stuff is endless and most things are not saving the world or humankind—just me and Christopher having fun and being together. Not much to ask you would think.

We both had at least a hundred-year plan for all the things we wanted to do together that included going a Winter Olympics for Christopher's love of skiing, the mountains and all things snowy, and our fascination of the bobsleigh that arose from watching the film *Cool Runnings* about fifty times. It would be an amazing trip.

Going to an Formula One race would have been fantastic and definitely on the list, although it would have to be done in style with full hospitality rather than sitting in a field, so obviously very expensive.

Generally, we wanted to travel everywhere together as Christopher loves exploring and, in a dream world, I would love for us to live by the sea in a cute cottage so we could go for walks on the beach and eat fresh seafood to our hearts' content and in the winter be snuggled up in front of an open fire, plus have a holiday home in the mountains.

Ideally, and something I was serious about trying to make work, was to scale down our work so we could ski for a few months each year as the mountains were where Christopher felt most at home and at peace.

However, unfortunately life is not like that and we received yet more devastating news about Christopher as the cancer had spread further and was at an advanced stage.

I think I was in denial and thought that as Christopher was so strong and fit that it would all be OK, and we would just carry on until finally a treatment would get rid of it. I'm sure he was thinking very differently but never let on. Such a strong man.

It was coming up to Christopher's fiftieth birthday, so I decided to arrange and surprise him with the best skiing holiday he had ever had in his life and invite his closest friends and family so we could all celebrate together and he would have the most amazing time and memories.

I did a lot of research and came up with a very smart place in Austria with a fabulous outside heated pool and set in a spectacular location.

Christopher's friends and brothers all agreed to come so, when I surprised him with my plan, he reacted with so much excitement, which was exactly the reaction I had hoped for. I let him know in plenty of time so he could look forward to the holiday and, during the run up, of course Christopher wanted all new gear which, naturally, is very expensive. However, as it was a big birthday, I helped pay for some new ski clothes and my dad offered to by some new skis that Christopher wanted to choose, revelling in the process of finding the perfect and latest model to suit his expert ability and then going to the shop to buy them.

Christmas passed and it was time to go skiing! A few of us all travelled together including our two best friends, Christina and Hadi, along with their young son, Sebastian who was always a delight and such an amazingly good child. Our friends love good food and wine so, as soon as we had checked in at the airport, they took us straight to the seafood bar and very kindly indeed treated us to a luxurious breakfast, including wine at ten a.m.!

We took the holiday transfer to the hotel which took about three hours up winding roads at which point I was doubting my choice of resort and getting nervous that the hotel would live up to the brochure pictures. We finally got there in the dark and, to my relief, walked into the most amazing, warm and welcoming hotel. It was fantastic. Our other friends and relatives came separately, some driving later and some had already arrived, so we were also greeted by familiar friendly faces.

We dumped our bags and went down for a later dinner in the very sleek and stylishly decorated but informal, warm and comfortable restaurant where we had a large table reserved for the ten of us for the duration of our stay. Our waiter, who was also with us for the duration, was really friendly and loved chatting to us all and, after a few days, was saving us the best wine in the house!

The next morning, we were up with the larks as Christopher was so excited as he just wanted to get out on the mountain. We had a couple of days to ski before his birthday so Christina, Hadi and I had a private lesson while Sebastian was in ski school. Two of our friends, including Bruce who had specially driven over from Munich where he had been working to be with Christopher, both skied with Christopher and they teamed up with our holiday rep as they got on so well and were all very competent skiers which is an understatement. Unfortunately, Fiona wasn't able to come as she had received some devastating family news which was really sad, so really lovely of Bruce to come on his own and very much appreciated. One of our friends spent her time in the spa as she didn't ski so it was really lovely of her to come. Christopher's brothers had also arrived but weren't skiing so went off exploring.

The morning of Christopher's birthday was so special. It was a sunny day with clear blue skies, sun and perfect snow. After I gave Christopher his card and a couple of small presents, we went for a quick but very hearty breakfast and all went off to do our separate things; the four boys on a special planned off-piste day including skiing over to Italy!

We all came back, not as early as you would have thought as Christopher wanted to get every last second on his skis, so we met in the town, still all in our ski boots and gear, and settled in a bar sitting outside with heaters and pumping music to have some well deserved après-ski. It was so lovely; all of us around a big wooden table with our faces red from the sun that day and worn out from all the exercise drinking hot *gluhwein* and ice-cold beers. The best feeling ever. Sebastian is the best behaved and loveliest child ever. He is so good and sat at the table with his juice just smiling and enjoying the laughter and stories of the day, one of which made the hairs on my neck stand up as Christopher and the boys, while off-piste in a really quiet area of woodland skiing through undisturbed snow, saw a large deer. It started running alongside Christopher while he was skiing as if he was running with him. So magical and he loved it.

Not wanting to get too carried away in the bar, we headed back to get showered and changed and back down for a birthday dinner. I had secretly reserved an outside area at the hotel which I decorated with banners and balloons and ordered some champagne for pre-dinner drinks for the big day, which all of Christopher's friends had also chipped in for which was so nice as I was quite broke at this point. Everyone was a bit surprised that I had done this outside, including Christopher, as I told him to put his coat back on to go down for drinks. However, it turned out to be so lovely as we were next to the heated pool with the clean air, snow and twinkling lights of the town and the mountains in the background, which was perfect. Once we had drunk all the champagne, which didn't take long, we went in for a very splendid dinner and, once again, some spectacular wine served by our waiter who was now our friend.

I'd asked the hotel to make a birthday cake (which turned out to be the nicest and healthiest cake I have ever eaten in my life, which was the icing on the cake so to speak), and when I nodded to the waiter to bring it out, the whole restaurant started singing 'Happy Birthday' to him. There was every nationality and age you could think of in the hotel restuarant and, as the drinks had been flowing, the sheer noise and overexcitment of the singing which went on for quite a while made the evening absolutely amazing. After dinner, the boys went out into town for more drinks and goodness knows what else, so I left them to it and retired to bed. I'm not sure what time Christopher came back, however, I know it was very late and he had consumed way too much alcohol but had the best time ever and still got up at seven a.m. and was still as excited as usual about going skiing that day.

Someone was looking down on us as the snow and the sun that week had never been better, and everyone had such a brilliant time.

The week ended and we all went back home, but the high from the fabulous week lasted a long time. We were back to normal with a bang, as the following months brought more horrendous operations and unbelievable pain and suffering for Christopher. Our friends, Christina and Hadi, very thoughtfully and very generously (which will never be forgotten), took us back to the ski resort we stayed at for Christopher's fiftieth for a long weekend to boost his spirits, which it did. However, when we came back it was obvious that he was really unwell and, later that year, lost his fight aged just fity. The most unfair thing in the whole world.

I can't actually describe, remember, or even want to remember, that day and the years that followed as it was all just a blur. I think I just went onto autopilot and got out of bed in the morning because that's what you do to keep going.

I eventually had to go back to work which, contrary to what people tell you, doesn't help by keeping your mind occupied. You just want to be in your own thoughts and your own time to try and make sense of things, although I have to say there was no rationalising any of what happened, as it was just horrific.

I had to ease myself back in gently as my events jobs were so full on and mentally demanding with the expectation of me being lively, funny and chatty, which was not what I felt like doing as my whole life – and the love of my life had gone. Although I needed to make up some money from not working much during the last few years wanting to be there for Christopher, I needed to take time off in between contracts to recover and regroup before I started a new one, so it was a balancing act of having enough money without stressing myself out even more.

Apart from work and going to the gym because that's what I had always done and I knew I needed to keep going for my head health as well as my body as it did make me feel better, I didn't go out anywhere as I just wanted to be in our home.

After three years, I did start to feel slightly differently, and the morning of my fiftieth birthday had arrived. I would normally love the birthday feeling as I somehow feel special and that the day ahead is going to be a great one. However, on this birthday, I had a real mix of emotions consisting of panic as I was half a century old which meant I had to dissect what I have done with my life so far, happiness as I've made if this far, but mainly immense sadness as it was three years since I lost the love of my life, my husband, Christopher, and he really should be here with me to celebrate but it was not to be.

Everyone seems to think a party is in order for a fiftieth, however, I plumped for a lunch in my favourite pub with my good old dad and Ellen, who are always there when I need them, plus another lunch with just a few family members and my friend, Christina, at a lovely fish restaurant which was perfect for me.

I also dragged my friend, Simone, to an opera in London as I had never been to one so I thought I had better try it. Unfortunately, I had oddly chosen a Shakspearean play turned into an opera which was not the best one to go and see as a first timer, as I didn't understand it even with the subtitles that were being shown and the stage set was, let's just say, very minimal, and did not change for the duration. Quite a few people did get up and walk out halfway through as I have to say the opera was not gripping by any means, but we stuck it out by having a few drinks in the intervals. At least I can say I have been.

So, fairly muted celebrations and completely different to what it would have been like if Christopher was still here with me.

Feeling quite old and still a bit lost at this point, I decided to buy myself a greenhouse and decked it out with lights, a lemon tree and a lavender plant on the wooden table that I had put in there so I could sit with a glass of wine and look out onto the garden. My place to retreat, a calming space with plants and surrounded by the garden birds, which I loved.

A lovely summer followed and over a month off in between jobs meant I could rekindle my love of the open water, so I spent a lot of time at my local lake; my friend Simone joining me at the weekends to go open water swimming.

The Windsor half marathon was coming around rapidly and, although I had achieved this once before having run it with Christopher, I really wanted to prove to myself I could do it again at the age of fifty, even with all the injuries I had sustained over time which had put pay to my running days for the previous couple of years.

I hadn't done anything about it and, with only a week to go before the half marathon, I decided I really wanted to do it and decided to book my place. I went out for one training run which was not good—painful and laboured—however, given I hadn't been running for a long time I was quite impressed I had managed to cover seven miles.

It took me a week to recover from that one run, so I thought I would decide on the day whether I would go for it or not. Of course, I didn't want to miss the opportunity and it was already paid for and it was such a nice day weather wise I decided to go for it. I booked a cab to get to the start line as parking was a nightmare, but the taxi got stuck in traffic so ended up having to get out and walk quite a way to even get to the start line.

What a lovely day and a lovely event. People were chatting to me on the way round and one really friendly girl asked if she could run with me for a bit as she liked my pace—slow! I got round the course; up the hills and through lovely scenery and thirteen point two miles and a very long time later, I crossed the finish line on a high and feeling very proud of my achievement even though my time was not great (but under three hours!).

I called Simone to tell her what I had just done and to see if she wanted to meet for coffee. She did ask me if I wanted to walk round to her house, which was about a twenty-minute walk, however, as I was hobbling with a painful hip, knee and foot I declined, so she very kindly came to pick me up and drove me home.

After that, I started to go out very occasionally with Simone. First for a few lunchtime drinks and then a bit more in the evening but by no means every week or even every month and, although I had a nice time, I didn't want to return to just going to the pub every weekend. Partly as I just didn't enjoy it as much as I used too and, although there were certain places to go where there were people of my own age, it just wasn't the same as it had been in the past, partly as I had turned into a complete lightweight and after a maximum of three drinks, I was quite squiffy so had horrendous hangovers for days and partly because it felt like I was going backwards, doing things I had done before meeting Christopher which I didn't want to do. Plus, there was the cost factor, as my work contracts were not back-to-back so I didn't have an abundance of spare cash.

So, I decided to just keep doing the things in my comfort zone... going to work, keeping fit and trying to do only the things I wanted to do. My 'things to try' list was getting shorter and shorter as I crammed so much into my younger years and I had actually done most things that I had ever wanted to do. Maybe I needed to find something more meaningful to try to give me a new focus, however, anything I thought of either seemed a bit too ambitious or unrealistic—or both.

How about a little shop or business and apartment in Zell am See, which would be amazing so I could spend time in the mountains which Christopher loved but I also love and, as Zell has a lake, I would have the best of both worlds for summer and winter. However, lack of funds will definitely put pay to that one but it will always be a dream of mine that I hope to achieve one day.

I do need to start thinking of my retirement which is slightly depressing and, as I don't have a plan and the years are creeping up on me, it is slightly scary.

I really can't keep doing my current job for another twenty years as its already taking its toll with the long hours and so much travelling and staying in different places. I now wake up a lot in the night in a panic, as I don't know where I am, so have to have a landing light on so I can quickly identify that I am in my own house, and now with the younger more ambitious people that are coming into the industry, it's much more competitive.

My eyesite is getting worse and, frankly, I'm a bit tired; but I am getting older so to be expected, I guess. I like watching *Gardeners' World* and going to bed early, but also, I don't want to be defeated by my aeging body and feel the need to take Christopher's lead and live every minute to the full. Even though it is not particularly appealing to do so without him here by my side.

I know everyone has their own problems and troubles in life, but some more than others. I guess it is the rough times that make or break you, so it is the most important time to make the right choices that drive you to make the most of and really enjoy the good times. I certainly appreciate everything much more than I did a few years ago, even down to everyday things in life, such as enjoying a warm sunny day when all the chores are done, going to the seaside for a day trip or even out for a long walk rounded off with a lovely lunch, which is my normal.

There are people around the world to whom normality is fighting for food and shelter, having experienced truly horrific things and really tough times that we can't even imagine, so the word, normal, is meaningless, but it is the simple things that I don't take for granted.

So finally, what are you doing still reading? Get out there and live life to the full. Enjoy your family and friends and cram in as much nice stuff as possible. Always give new things a go as you never know when things may change.

Life is too short, and do we really know, or should we actually really care, what everyone else is doing and what actually is seen as 'normal'? We should all just be nice to each other, do our best with what we have and, most of all, be happy.

I can't ever expect to be as happy as I was with someone as amazing as Christopher, but I can hope to be happy again and will try to only do the things I like, that make me happy. However, I'm aware that the are years rolling on, so what is next for me?

Maybe I should, *Try Something New at 50…*